The Harvest

*Timeless
Lessons
for an
Abundant
Life*

AlexSandra Lett

Lett's set a spell...

The Harvest

Timeless Lessons
for an Abundant Life

First Edition, Paperback, Copyright © 2015
ISBN-13: 978-0-9970324-0-6
First Edition, Hardcover, Copyright © 2015
ISBN-13: 978-0-9970324-1-3
Second Edition, Paperback, Copyright © 2015
ISBN-13: 978-0-9970324-2-0
Kindle Edition, Copyright © 2015
ISBN-13: 978-0-9970324-3-7

© 2015 AlexSandra Lett

Published by

TRANFORMATIONS

1996 Buckhorn Road
Sanford, NC 27330-9782 • USA

LettsSetaSpell@aol.com
www.atimelessplace.com

For more information contact:

AlexSandra "Sandy Lynn" Lett
919-258-9299

The Harvest
is dedicated
to readers of my nostalgia
"Lett's Set a Spell" column,
which was first created in 2000.

Publication of this book celebrates
15 years of my sharing stories
and offering reflections
about a way of living and giving
through several generations.

Thank you readers for inspiring me
to keep on writing!

The Harvest

Timeless Lessons
for an Abundant Life

Timeless Lessons for an Abundant Life

Growing crops is not for sissies…it requires planning and persistence every day of the year because sowing seeds and expecting a harvest calls for total commitment. This means working hard, maintaining faith, honoring cycles, taking risks, sharpening the saw, and functioning as a team.

Running a country store involves keeping up with supply and demand to meet the needs of folks in a community…providing fuel and food and more while also offering a place for sharing stories and connecting with neighbors.

Leaving the farm and starting a business takes guts and calls for a combination of charming personality, risk-taking, and unwavering belief in oneself and the products and services offered to customers.

Working hard I learned lessons while growing up on a big farm in rural North Carolina from my parents who cultivated crops, raised animals, gathered tons of vegetables, fruits from our large garden, and apples, peaches, and pecans from trees in our yard.

Listening intently I learned lessons at my Grandpa's country store where he offered staples like "dranks" and MoonPies, hoop cheese, and cookies and candy from large jars on the counter. Here we took a break from constant chores and tedious hours to share stories and catch up on the latest gossip.

Introduction

Watching carefully I learned lessons from my favorite uncle about a burning desire and big dreams as he developed a small cabinet shop into a large building supply company. Through his attitude and actions I saw there were possibilities beyond the family farm.

From many folks I learned a lot about being honest, having values, developing character, respecting traditions, cultivating a sense of humor, establishing harmonious relationships, and meeting the needs of family and others. Bountiful crops, stocked shelves, and big businesses showed me that success is possible in many different ways if we are willing to pay the price.

Perhaps my greatest teachers were Mother Nature and Father Time as I discovered how to live in harmony with flavors of the fields, seasons of the year, and matters of the heart. The Creator spoke to me most when I was roaming the woods or sitting still by the pond, which inspired me to write poetry and prose.

My childhood in Buckhorn community was humble, which was typical of farm life in the 1950s and 1960s where most folks owned plenty of land but were cash poor. The "citified" life attracted me with its fancy dress shops and impressive homes in suburbia. I confess that I wanted fame and fortune. Eventually I experienced notoriety through careers in the media and in marketing, and later through writing and publishing books, but there was always a longing for something more.

Introduction

I couldn't find fulfillment out there in the world. Making a lot of money and providing communication services for eager clients and customers did not make me feel rich inside. Getting more attention from loyal readers and appreciative audiences convinced me that I offered entertaining and educational programs, but it was not enough. Coming home and making peace with my childhood helped for a while but also exposed wounds that needed to be healed and reminded me of truths that could not be revealed.

Through the decades I shared humorous anecdotes, interesting reflections, spiritual solutions, and practical strategies with all types of people. I met the needs of others in many incarnations, but somewhere along the way I lost touch with my divine mission.

Finally it took an overwhelming car accident and devastating failure to stop the insanity that had taken over my life and bring me to my knees and say "God, I surrender...use me."

While healing my body and mind of pain and trauma I also soothed my spirit and eventually began to understand that my soul was revealing a deeper purpose for my life. As I sowed seeds for growing and reaping a different me, I had to go back to the beginning and fully appreciate the lessons I had learned to create an abundant life.

*To everything
there is a season.
A time for every purpose
under heaven.
A time to be born,
and a time to die;
A time to plant,
and a time to reap
what is planted.*

Ecclesiastes 3:1, 2

1
Rise and Shine

"Rise and shine!"

Daddy yelled these words at the top of his lungs as he quickly entered the bedroom I shared with my sister before the crack of dawn, even before the rooster crowed. He happily proceeded with the whining words of a made-up song. Wearing his faded and stained navy blue overalls, he was raring to go.

My sister Mary Carolyn, my brother Jimmy Doyle, and I walked trancelike to the kitchen table, eyes half open, numb with fatigue from having worked our fingers to the bone the day before. The smell of baked bread and greasy meat was intoxicating. The aroma of perfectly-brewed coffee wafting through the air was all-too-familiar when the old wood stove was fired up for hours.

"Hurry up and eat your breakfast!"

Mama's high voice cracked the morning silence like a drill sergeant's. As she scurried around the kitchen and prepared leftover biscuits and meat for farm helpers, Mama would say, "I do more before breakfast than you 'young'uns' do all day long."

When we saw the big spread on the kitchen table – freshly made biscuits, scrambled eggs, ham, sausage, red-eye gravy, and grits plus homemade blackberry and apple jelly from the pantry – we never doubted her word. If we kids didn't care for plain milk, she would stir in Hershey's cocoa to make it taste like chocolate, and if we wanted Coca-Cola for breakfast, that was OK, too.

It's Tobacco Time

This was typical of a summer day in the 1960s...and anything but jubilant. It was tobacco time...calling for 4 a.m. risings, necessary to take cured tobacco out of the barn before priming new tobacco, handing it, looping it on sticks, and putting more into the barn.

We kids had no right to complain...Mama (Ruby Lett) had been cooking for hours, and Daddy (Bud Lett) had been up and down all night firing tobacco barns. He had turned the heat off on one barn the day before, and while golden cured tobacco leaves cooled, we slept. Now it was time to transfer tobacco to the pack house, which was an old abandoned church on our farm. Stacks of tobacco already piled high decorated the large room that once held a congregation, but there was always space for more dried leaves.

Puttin' in tobacco was an exhausting experience for several months on this farm in the heart of North Carolina. After taking cured tobacco out of the barn we divided up the labor to handle the main task of the day: filling the empty barn up with freshly primed green tobacco. The men and boys of Buckhorn community headed for the field, and womenfolk and children took their places at the barn.

The barn was Queen Bee Ruby's hive, and she kept us worker bees a-buzzin'. While hollerin' orders she talked a mile a minute. One day Mama was yackin' non-stop when a fly came under the barn shelter and headed straight for her wide-open mouth. Mama spit it out and complained "Ooo...a fly flew right in my mouth."

Mack Griffin, a neighbor, concluded, "Well, if a fly came under the shelter, there won't no where else it could go." We all laughed so hard we almost peed our pants, and Mama kept right on talking.

Daddy was foreman in the field where he primed the fastest and scurried the farthest down the rows while keeping everyone chuckling. He reminded workers: "The early bird gets the worm."

Here Daddy was chief comedian – he would laugh hysterically at himself, and his humor was contagious. As usual, he loved to recall tall tales and dramatize the same crazy stories and funny jokes over and over again.

Sleds glided down narrow rows, led by mules who knew that "get up" meant to go forward about 50 feet and "whoa" told them to stop for loading. After the sleds carried the tobacco to the barn, workers unloaded it on a long bench.

We "handers" gathered fresh green leaves into bundles and gave it to "loopers," who firmly and artistically wrapped the tobacco on sticks. These sticks were carried to the barn and passed to a man – usually a brave one with long legs who would hang the tobacco high on the tier poles and maybe even fight off the   occasional snake who liked the warmth and darkness and wanted to nest there.

One thing I disliked about tobacco was the gum residue. When we took tobacco off the sled and handed it to a "looper," we got gluey gum all over our hands that was hard to remove. Others laughed when I wore old white cotton gloves discarded from church clothes, but when I took off the gloves my hands were "purrty," and other folks were out there scrubbing off the gum at the well.

Sowing and Reaping Tobacco

Setting out tobacco plants

Walking in tobacco fields

Inspecting green tobacco in fields

Passing tobacco after looping on stick

Driving the tractor

Priming tobacco in fields

Putting wood in tobacco barn for curing

Bidding on tobacco at market

This is the farmhouse where Bud and Ruby Lett moved in 1947 and raised three "young-uns," Jimmy Doyle, Mary Carolyn, and Sandy Lynn.

Rest for the Weary

When the tobacco farm was full of tobacco family members and some helpers gratefully headed for the small kitchen in our farmhouse, fondly called "Ruby's Restaurant," where Mama quickly fixed hamburgers, hot dogs, and French fries. We girls sliced onions, tomatoes, and cucumbers fresh from the garden, got out the homemade pickles Mama had canned last year, set the table, and later cleaned up the dishes.

Afterwards, during the heat of the day, we stayed out of the sun. Sometimes Carolyn and I ironed clothes, even our bed linens, that Mama had hung out on the line after running them through the old ringer washing machine on the back porch. We loved to fall into sweet slumber during the heat of the day or perhaps catch the latest episode of *As the World Turns* and *The Guiding Light*. There really was rest for the weary!

As the earth cooled, we left the comforts of couch and fan and tended to other crop chores or gathered garden pickin's for cooking and canning.

If we were lucky after supper we would walk across the road to Grandpa's country store where farmers compared tobacco progress and crop yields and wives shelled peas for tomorrow's supper. We young'uns listened intently because stories and gossip ranked above television shows and brought relief to our fatigue.

On Sundays Lett family members honored the Sabbath by attending services at Moore Union Congregational Christian Church and many continue to do so. It is no longer named Congregational just Christian.

There was one day of the week we never worked, and that was the Sabbath. Our family of five ate breakfast, donned our nicest clothes, and headed for Sunday School and preachin' services at Moore Union Congregational Christian Church four miles down the road. Daddy fussed but traded his overalls for a suit and tie because Mama said so. She often commented, "Church is the home of the Lord and we will look our best."

It was Mama who didn't get to rest much because she got up early and started cooking two meats and several pots of vegetables. We invited the minister and his family for Sunday dinner at least once a month, and if other neighbors wanted to stop by that was OK too. There was always plenty of fixins'…including fried chicken…at Ruby's Restaurant.

Religion was very important in our home and community, and we read The Bible almost every day. More importantly we lived in harmony with the Golden Rule: "Do unto others as you would have them do unto you" from Luke 6:31 when Jesus was talking about the importance of loving your enemies. We were told to treat others the way we would want to be treated.

Our lives on the Lett family farm were filled with hard work but soft hearts as we came together as a team sowing and reaping in tune with the seasons of the year.

Lessons Learned

On the farm we lived in tune with the cycle of sowing and reaping and in harmony with Mother Nature and the seasons of the year. We followed *The Bible's* teachings about honoring the Sabbath.

While early risings were painful for us kids, this phase of the growing season only lasted a few weeks. Getting up before others became a practice in my everyday life that helped me excel in school and work activities. Even in high school, after getting off the bus, I would take a short nap and recharge before cheerleading at a ballgame or attending a yearbook staff meeting. Now I get up early, have a protein drink for breakfast because a heavy meal bogs me down, work several hours, then eat lunch and take a nap before going to my computer or out to a meeting.

It took me a while to appreciate the attitude of both my parents who enjoyed hard work and planned ahead so that each stage of the sowing and reaping season went smoothly. They set goals and determined objectives then took action to make sure they accomplished what they had set out to do. Others benefited tremendously from their results. As Mama would say when we children argued about the constant chores: "Just do it!"

Questions

What lessons did you learn from your family while growing up?

How have their habits and attitudes affected the way you work and live today?

What seeds have you planted throughout your life that are now ready to be harvested?

Are you ready and prepared to do what it takes to reap what you've sown?

*The early bird
gets the worm.*

If you do follow your bliss,
you put yourself on a track that
has been there all the while,
waiting for you, and the life
that you ought to be living
is the one you are living.
When you can see that,
you begin to meet people
who are in the field of your bliss,
and they open doors to you.
I say follow your bliss and
don't be afraid,
and doors will open where
you didn't know they were going to be.

Joseph Campbell and the Power of Myth,
Public Broadcasting System (PBS)
interview with Bill Moyers

2
Bliss and Blisters

Early in life I figured out that Daddy and Mama believed hard work was considered the top priority on our family's farm. In late January every year when the moon was just right, Daddy and Mama and we young'uns would make a beeline to the plant bed where tobacco seeds were placed tenderly under cold hard soil. This was a sure sign that the new growing season had begun.

Sowing seeds with the expectation of reaping a harvest became the first lesson I learned about farming. Later, I realized that I could use this message for taking crucial steps to succeed in the arts, in business, in relationships, and every aspect of life.

One neighbor discovered that if he set out his beet seeds in the plant bed about the same time, they grew a little faster than the tobacco so they would eventually lift the protective sheet over the bed higher, creating growing space for budding tobacco sprouts. Unique approaches to routine practices became a metaphor for my interest in trying new things beyond the family farm.

Tobacco as Main Money Crop

Tobacco was considered our main money crop, and its harvest included various stages of labor from sowing the seeds in winter to taking the cured leaves to market in late summer and early fall. Even though we kids conducted constant chores, we eventually figured out that we were better at some things than others.

Some say growing tobacco was like starting a second religion because it was discussed as much or more so than worshiping God. For many farmers, the tobacco crop's earnings became their salvation because profits provided the steady income to modernize the house, acquire citified equipment, and above all, buy food and supplies not available on the farm.

When the small plants that had been transplanted from the seedbeds began to flower, folks snapped the buds from the top of the plant. In turn, other buds, called suckers, developed further down the plant and had to be pulled off by hand. Farmers insisted on topping and suckering and enlisted us children for these grueling tasks. Daddy said removing suckers allowed all the nutrients to go to the leaves and caused the plant to grow longer into the summer. Crawling down tobacco rows and pulling off suckers instigated blisters on my knees and hands.

Getting rid of those awful suckers was a difficult task but made the tobacco plants thrive, and meanwhile I learned a lesson about doing what is best for the crop and the team. Also I realized that sometimes in life we must get rid of things like suckers that do not serve us…including people, especially troublesome boyfriends, but don't get me started on that subject!

Daddy's Blisters and Bliss

Daddy especially enjoyed raising tobacco, nurturing the seeds he placed in the plant bed, tending the tall green stalks until they could be cured in barns, and adoring the golden leaves he loaded on pickup trucks for the market. When Daddy dug his fingers deep into the soil, he seemed to gather energy and power from Mother Earth. Like a prince on the palace grounds, Daddy admired the fields lush with rows of green. Daddy's love of the land nourished his soul. On the Lett farm Bud Lett found his kingdom.

The fruits of Daddy's labor provided blessings for many people. His watermelon crop was a spiritual ministry…nothing delighted him more than filling my car with red and yellow varieties for me to distribute to friends. Daddy planted apple, peach, pear, and pecan trees and blueberry bushes so he could relish their growth and yield and have more treasures to share with others. He found pleasure in growing vegetables and fruits, treating each bean from the garden, fruit from a tree, or berry from a bush like a gem from a mine.

Bliss and Blisters

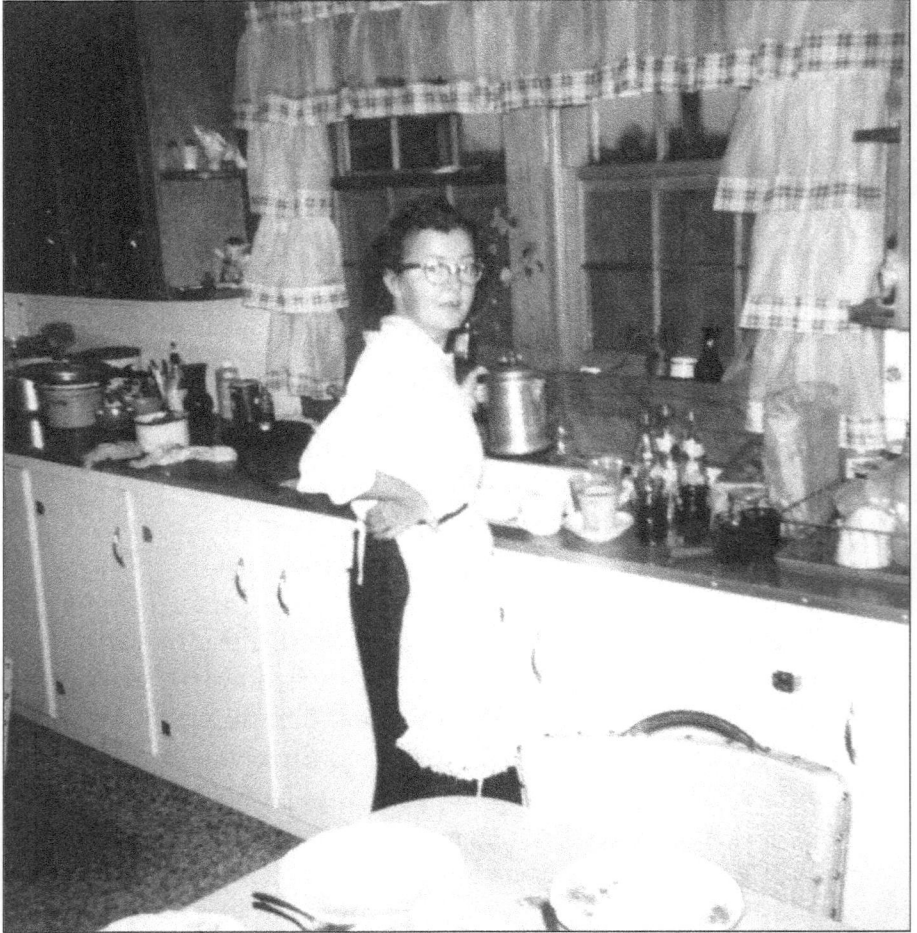

Mama poses for a picture in 1960 in her kitchen,
which we fondly referred to as Ruby's Restaurant.

Daddy shows off
a large sweet potato
he dug out of his field;
below, he is surrounded
by watermelons
he grew in his garden.

Mama Ruled Ruby's Restaurant

Meanwhile, Mama perfected her culinary concoctions by standing over a hot stove daily   so that Daddy, family, and friends could relish the many delicious delights from her kitchen. Just as the tobacco crop peaked so did the garden, and the whole family pitched in to pick tomatoes, shell peas, snap beans, shuck corn, and help Mama with canning and freezing fruits and vegetables.

When Mama cooked in the kitchen she reigned like a queen of dining. In Ruby's Restaurant, she was the chef, the hostess, and the waitress. She excitedly fed her guests pleasure and joy as well as favorite foods, such as fried chicken, mashed potatoes, green beans, fried corn bread, coconut pies, and plain cake. Folks constantly praised her cookin'. In her kitchen Mama felt passion and pride.

Mama's food fixin's and Daddy's garden pickin's were always greeted with appreciation because they featured a flavor and an aroma that went beyond all expectations. Through their love of labor Mama and Daddy experienced life's most powerful secret: to work to his or her heart's content.

Feeding the Animals

While I detested most of the everyday chores that never ended, I discovered that my favorite task on the farm was nourishing the animals. We were blessed with lots of food and plenty of leftovers so first I fed the dogs and cats…sometimes a dozen. These precious pets liked the meats, gravies, dumplings, and sweet corn, even eating it off the cob. We never gave them packaged products.

Next I served treats to the chickens who preferred vegetables and fruits to their cornmeal. Finally I fed the pigs who would eat anything chewable on the planet and gobbled down household scraps commonly called slop and their store-bought grain mixture.

Mama said I was prone to day-dreaming as I resisted the daily duties and hard labor required to raise animals, grow produce, and harvest crops. When I took breaks during tasks like setting out tobacco, pulling weeds, pickin' peas, or gathering corn, I learned to banter with the folks who taunted me about being lazy. As a teenager I'd quip: "I ain't lazy...I just ain't found a suitable occupation yet."

Even then I had a notion that sometime in the future I would find enjoyable work that developed my talents, fostered creativity, honored my heart's desire, and brought joy to my spirit.

Years later I read mythologist Joseph Campbell's famous quote "Follow your bliss," intended to inspire individuals to be true to themselves...to courageously break free of a life of mediocrity and instead choose vision, creativity, passion, and excitement. However, when Campbell saw this phrase misinterpreted as self-serving permission to chase immediate pleasures that produced pain for many people, he remarked, "I should have said follow your blisters."

Mama and Daddy knew that a long time ago...

Lessons Learned

While constant chores every day of the week and physical labor through the months became overwhelming at times, we consistently saw the results of our commitment. I confess that sometimes when I was outdoors whether suckering tobacco or hanging out with the pigs, I would look around me at the trees and acres of crops and feel a sense of connection with the land and its beauty during every season of the year. Sometimes I felt closer to God while in nature than I did in church.

I didn't understand then that when growing tobacco, other crops, and garden pickin's, my parents were co-creating with God and living in tune with loving labor and bringing forth gifts from the soil.

Through the years I noticed that Mama and Daddy never complained about their duties on the farm because they had made their choice to follow in the footsteps of both sets of parents…and they were proud of being farmers. They worked as partners and encouraged others to be part of their team.

Questions

What do you love to do so much that you wouldn't mind dealing with a few blisters to experience your bliss?

What could you and God be co-creating together?

3
Meeting Needs

After dealing with lack of bare essentials during the Depression, Recession, World War I, and World War II, my grandfather, the late Willie Puzie Lett – called "Captain Puzie" – vowed to never deal with shortages again. He wanted to know that he would also have kerosene on hand for lighting stoves for cooking and heating and gas for running his pick-up truck.

"When I had money for gas I couldn't buy it and when gas was for sale I didn't have the money," Grandpa told me.

In 1946 he and kinfolk and some neighbors erected a two-room building for a country store. Rumor has it that folks came from miles away to help with the construction project, saying they might as well fix up a store. They compared it with a barn-raising, and they raised the roof after cutting the wood, hammering nails, and building walls. Some say their excitement had something to do with the "corn likker" being passed from hand to hand. For you city slickers, this is slang for moonshine!

Grandpa (Willie Puzie Lett) stands behind the counter at his country store where he is weighing hoop cheese on the scales.

Grandpa's Country Store

Captain Puzie, who was born in 1888, opened Lett's Grocery and Filling Station on our 400-acre farm in Buckhorn community just four miles outside the city limits of a little town called Broadway and 12 long miles from Sanford, the county seat of Lee County located in the heart of North Carolina. At Grandpa's country store he could provide kerosene, also known as lamp oil, for lighting lamps and stoves and fuel for vehicles and a wide variety of foods. Customers could buy staples like bread, flour, sugar, and lard and snacks like "Nabs" and MoonPies and "dranks " like RC Colas and NeHi's.

These soft drinks were considered good for body and soul, but folks talked about those wayward sots who were "bad to drank," a gentle way of saying they had the habit of drinking too many alcoholic beverages. Heaven help anyone who was described as "drunk as a skunk" because he could be pert-near burned at the stake by the old potbellied stove in the back room or condemned to hell under the store's shelter. These two meeting places were the closest thing to Judgment Day in the Buckhorn community.

On chilly days and nights local folks would hang out around Grandpa's potbellied stove to catch up on the latest gossip. On summer evenings farmers would "shoot the breeze" outside where they compared tobacco prices and crop yields while wives shelled peas for tomorrow's supper.

Grandpa's country store opened in 1946 and was officially named
Lett's Grocery and Filling Station.

"Setting a spell" was what they called it…this had nothing to do with witchcraft – it was about sitting down and staying awhile. However, if one "set" long enough at the country store Grandpa would talk long and hard about chasing the Devil out of some evil folks who didn't live up to the standards of these tow-the-line Christian folks.

Outrageous people spinning yarns and sharing stories came in and out of the store from the crack of dawn to bedtime. Grandpa was sometimes nippy, could even be high as a kite, but don't tell anyone this family secret! Whatever his mood he loved preaching a sermon from his self-erected pulpit – a stack of Coca-Cola and Pepsi crates at the country store. Grandpa's colorful personality and his strong views on religion, education, crops, and politics were main attractions for customers.

The country store was the social center of Buckhorn community where farmers, neighbors, and passersby could chew the fat right off their gums and double dribble their lips until they were slap-dab worn-out. The men loved to gossip more than anything in the world while the women compared notes on goings-on and often said, "Well, bless her heart."

They knew their neighbor's lives like they did their own – from the wasp sting on the foot to the gall bladder removed. When cancer ate right through to the bone and snuffed out a light in the community, they mourned like it was their own flesh and blood.

Customs Better Than Change

Grandpa's country store was not just their second home – it was where part of their heart resided. Here folks could feel a security that can only be experienced when routine is the core of one's existence. The humdrum that might bore the "citified" to tears brought reassurance for conventional country folks. They were comfortable that their mates and young'uns were either within hollerin' distance or at home on the farm.

Day in and day out, Grandpa bent my ear with his tales of the good ole days and how wonderful they were. I couldn't tell what part he liked best…walking barefoot with snow between the toes fighting frostbite because shoes were a luxury they couldn't afford or turning off oil lamps early 'cause there "weren't no money for oil." Why he preferred freezing feet and dark houses to warmth and lights is beyond me, but for Grandpa robotic habits were better than getting used to anything new. Tradition was more comfortable than change – he feared progress more than the Plague.

Grandpa didn't know about the Amish but through some strange biological mutation he had inherited their genes 'cause he thought electricity was a total waste and distrusted new-fangled gadgets like tractors. The Bible says the sins of our fathers are passed on 'cause my Daddy…also named Puzie…got those same genes and hated change even more than his namesake.

Modern-day psychologists say most people tend to repeat the mistakes of their ancestors unless they experience a dramatic wake-up call, a major intervention that forces them to choose another course. That's what happened to me, but we'll talk about that later.

In 1970 "Sandy Lynn" hangs out with her Grandpa
who was fondly called "Captain Puzie" by customers.

Grandpa's Passion and Platform

Grandpa made money at the country store. Being the sole proprietor was his passion and his platform for sharing stories and allowing others to enjoy a welcome diversion from constant chores. When a neighbor opened a country store Grandpa noted, "I started my store to meet needs and make a living...Sydney is trying to make a killing."

Grandpa's sidekick was his daughter Gladys who married young but didn't like her husband so came back home to raise her "young'uns" at Grandpa's house. Everyone called her "Aunt Gla-dees" and many considered her Grandma Lett since Grandpa's wife Verta had died in 1951. Aunt Gladys was highly praised for her mothering, cooking, and quilting. Like my parents she depended on tobacco as her main source of income but didn't have many expenses because Grandpa owned the house and they paid cash for everything, even cars and trucks.

As a child I did not share the excitement Grandpa felt when crates of "dranks," cartons of cigarettes, and boxes of staples arrived regularly at his country store across the road. I took for granted the sparkle in Aunt Gladys' eyes as she pointed out the many fabrics in her various quilt designs.

Back then I did not understand the passion in my Daddy's face as he walked the fields, bragged about crop yields, and took the tobacco to market. I could not comprehend the pride in my Mama's smile when she showed off a cake straight from the oven or displayed jars of freshly canned green beans.

During my childhood I did not know that I was surrounded by artists who naturally created masterpieces and by entrepreneurs who constantly celebrated their wares. Daddy, Mama, Grandpa, and Aunt Gladys discovered the secret to life: passion for their work and a sense of purpose. These four role models, who were very different in talent and temperament, had one thing in common: each chose the work best suited for their skills and dispositions and performed their tasks with love.

Lett's Grocery and Filling Station was the backdrop for a quiet, sensitive little girl who enjoyed the constant yakking, tall tales, and juicy gossip at the country store and who grew up to become a writer. I learned a lot about farming and living from listening carefully to conversations, stored information in my brain, and recorded my observations out of a deep need to understand people, their personalities, and myself in relation to them.

Find a need and fill it.

– Motto of Ruth Stafford Peale,
wife of the Reverend Norman Vincent Peale
author of *The Power of Positive Thinking*

Lessons Learned

While the Lett farm was acquired because of its rich soil and the whole family farmed, at age 58 Grandpa broke with his custom of resisting change and cut back on hard labor. After all, his son Bud had returned from war to be in charge of growing crops. Grandpa opened a business that would supply essentials for the farm and a few luxuries for his family and customers. This enterprise also suited him better because he had the gift of gab and would entertain as well as serve customers. Grandpa discovered a new passion that fueled his ability to tell stories, used his sense of humor, and satisfied his need to be in charge.

Lett's Grocery and Filling Station offered a focal point where folks could connect with others, a nice respite from many hours of labor, a great source of information about farming and living, and an opportunity to create relationships and build a sense of community. I didn't know until much later that this was a form of networking and making contacts personally and professionally.

Questions

What changes would you need to make to align with your creative desires to achieve your deepest dream?

Can you give up who you are today to become a higher version of yourself?

Are you using lack of experience or abundance of age as an excuse not to use your talents, move forward, and pursue your deepest dream?

4
Choices Beyond the Farm

When we were growing up we were told over and over that it was easier for a camel to pass through the eye of a needle than a rich man to get to Heaven. Poverty was a virtue, THEY said, and if we coveted citified possessions then we were probably possessed by the Devil himself. I never did figure out who THEY were.

Religion was about loving the Lord and others, living by the Good Book, and raising young'uns in the way of righteousness. Anything else was just a wayward way of worshipping Satan's gold, according to many folks in rural settings.

However, through the years as some of the kinfolks accumulated elaborate houses, fancy cars and big companies, the family began to look at money differently – especially when one of our own became available to loan money for buying houses, starting businesses, and writing big checks to the home church.

That's what happened with my Daddy's only brother Gilbert and nary a soul in the family, Buckhorn community or throughout the entire state of North Carolina would dare question Uncle Gilbert's ability to get into heaven! In fact, folks believed Gilbert would be driving his Rolls Royce straight through the pearly gates when Judgment Day comes.

Gilbert was nicknamed "Shine" because of his bright blonde hair. Perhaps this was a sign that he was a golden child, destined to become a shining star. It was hard for Gilbert to shine on the farm though because he just couldn't seem to please Grandpa, not that anyone could, mind you.

Take cotton, for instance, Gilbert just didn't "cotton to" it at all. "My brother and every one of my sisters picked 200 pounds a day, and I worked just as hard but only got half that much," Gilbert said.

Back then schooling was not at the top of the list for farm families, but the local boys and girls went to a two-room schoolhouse called Hickory Level to learn to read and write. They walked a mile there and back. After Gilbert finished first grade, this country school was annexed into the school system and the teacher made him repeat first grade to catch up with the other kids from the bigger and better school. Later he was held back another grade, which put him in the same room with his sister Selma. "That shed a bad light on my life, making me a second class student," he admitted to me.

That incident was the straw that broke the camel's back for Gilbert – and he dropped out of school after sixth grade at age 14 and went to work full-time on the farm. He really tried to do well but his heart wasn't in it, and restlessness was brewing inside him. "I realized at age of 18, farming wasn't my cup of tea," he said.

Second Son Rejects Farming

After a steamy argument with Grandpa, Gilbert rolled up his extra pair of overalls and shirt and left for greener pastures. Rumor has it Grandpa was yelling "You'll never amount to anything" as Gilbert was packing to leave. Grandpa just had to run things in the ground.

When Gilbert walked away from the familiar house and farm he weighed only 130 pounds but was heavy with determination to try something different. This turned out to be a life-changing decision, which led Gilbert to finding his own place in the sun. Sure enough, it wasn't in farming.

He went to stay with his sister Cleo and her husband Carlyle in nearby Lillington and started doing public work. His first job was working at a saw mill and then later operating a fork lift. When Gilbert saw one of Cleo's neighbors, Isabelle Patterson, it was love at first sight, and the courting began.

In March 1943 Gilbert received his draft notice and was scheduled for a physical examination. He and Isabelle were planning to marry after she graduated from high school but while riding to Dillon, S.C. with friends who were getting hitched, they decided to marry too, in case he was called to serve in World War II. As it turned out he was rejected due to a hernia and hearing loss so happily focused on finding out what his talents were.

Gilbert took a job at a food distributing company, earning $25 a week for 50 hours. He started off as a warehouse loader but did whatever was necessary – even if it meant sweeping the floor after he punched out to keep his job. Eventually he got into driving the delivery truck and selling some of their products. He took a second job for extra income – after getting home from work he sold concessions during second shift at Edwards Motor Company, which manufactured airplane parts to supply armed forces during the war. Since he didn't have a car yet he walked to work, then back home, took a nap, and later took his food wagon through the plant again at midnight to accommodate the third shift workers. He sold sandwiches, soft drinks, candy and cigarettes – this was long before vending machines, mind you. This moonlighting venture added another $30 to his weekly pay.

As war activities decreased, Edwards Company closed down and so did his concession stand. Gilbert took a job as route salesman for Pepsi-Cola, delivering 640 cases a week. He could have sold three times more but sugar rations curtailed production. Later he bought a distributorship for Swensen Foods and began selling the newest staples in the American diet – peanuts, potato chips, nabs, etc. Gilbert discovered that he had the gift of gab and could easily communicate with people.

The turning point in Gilbert's life came at age 30 when he and investors bought a cabinet shop, and he became general manager. His native intelligence, his hard work, and his captivating personality led to the creation of a large building supply store Lee Builder Mart and additional branches in nearby towns.

Gilbert and his wife Isabelle had two children, a son Tony and daughter Janice who became my favorite cousins. On holidays our two families gathered together and looked forward to a big celebration on Christmas Eve. Going to the family's new house on a lake shaped my views about money.

Since I shared a small bedroom with my sister without even a table to do my homework or a closet…just a wardrobe and cedar chest…I was enchanted when I walked into Janice's bedroom and saw her canopy bed, dresser, chest of drawers, and dressing table, cream trimmed in gold. It looked like the resting place for a princess. Tony's room was impressive too…it featured built-in wood cabinets with bookcases, a desk, and large workspace. From then on I vowed I would be citified one day and live in a house like that.

When I visited Uncle Gilbert's cabinet shop and later the large building supply store I realized that owning a prosperous business can lead to a more materialistic lifestyle with luxuries.

Family Memories

Cousins Jimmy, Tony, Carolyn, Janice, and Sandy Lynn
celebrate Christmas Eve at the farmhouse in 1959.

Jimmy, Carolyn, and Sandy Lynn
pose for an official portrait in 1953.

Mama and Daddy relax at the new home of Aunt Isabelle and Uncle Gilbert
after a holiday meal in 1963.

Carolyn and Sandy Lynn enjoy spending time with Janice and Tony
beside their "citified" Christmas tree in 1963.

Gilbert Becomes Master Builder

Gilbert was a role model for many people including me. As he built places he also developed people…he inspired others to grow. He taught his son Tony, daughter Janice and son-in-law Art and employees they were not just selling supplies, but constructing buildings and contributing to the lives of people and the community. He helped many people make their dreams of owning a home come true.

As the Sanford area grew with the influx of companies and the development of a large country club and a big upscale neighborhood, Gilbert's business expanded rapidly.

As Gilbert's bank account grew his sphere of influence increased. He gave money to his home church and donated building supplies, time, and money to people and projects hither and yon. Big checks to the local college provided scholarships for deserving nursing students and led to the Lett name on a building.

In Broadway, near the school where he felt he wasn't up to par as a student, stands Lett Family Park, located on Gilbert Lett Road, so named because of his donation of nine acres. This park is an arena for ballgames and sports activities.

If Grandpa were alive today he'd be yelling from the rooftop about his mighty fine son, and admitting that sure enough, Shine did amount to something!

Gilbert Lett stands in front of his large building supply store
Lee Builder Mart in 1963.

Lessons Learned

While Gilbert figured out he was not good at farming like his Daddy and brother he bravely discovered his unique gifts. Eventually he did follow in Grandpa's footsteps by starting his own business. Both men served as examples of the entrepreneurial approach to earning a living.

Gilbert's actions and generosity also helped change the country folks' distrust of wealth and demonstrated to the family and others that money can be used to for good…to build houses, people, and lives.

As I watched Gilbert I realized that sometimes a person has to reject the old way of life to pursue their passions. Through experimenting, working hard, being persistent, and acquiring lots of blisters, Gilbert eventually found his bliss.

Questions

What kind of risks are you willing to take to discover your talents and pursue your passions?

What negative belief systems prevent you for focusing on being successful?

What behaviors and actions do you need to change to go for your deepest dreams?

Gilbert shows off his Rolls Royce.

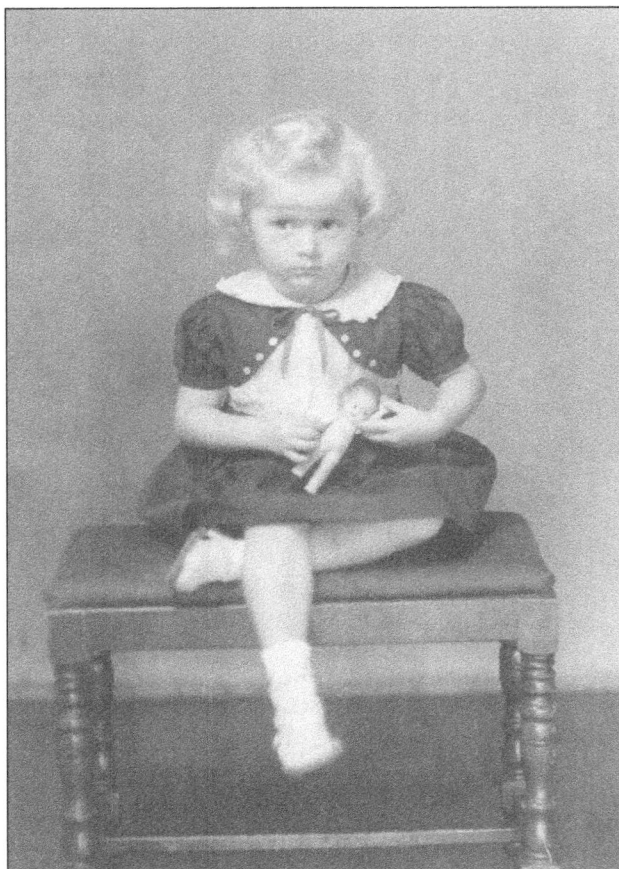

Sandy Lynn holds a favorite toy doll when she poses
for a picture at the Olen Mills Studio in 1953.

5
Be True to Yourself

Mama said I was an angelic child, quiet and shy, who could play alone contentedly for hours with my dolls and their clothes. She said that when my brother Jimmy and sister Carolyn were at school she would forget I was even there.

As I grew up, however, I began to explore new ideas and do things my way, which didn't set too well with my Mama's controlling personality. She took her role as Mother Hen very seriously and didn't want any of her biddies straying too far from the nest, either physically or mentally.

Meanwhile Daddy took a spare-the-rod, spoil-the-child approach with us three young'uns. Like most country folk Daddy expected his children to follow in his footsteps. He had trouble accepting me because I was "quar" (meaning queer or strange) and down-right peculiar with all my weird ideas, highfalutin' notions, and citified interests.

Mama and Daddy hollered "Sandy Lynn" in a shrill voice when I didn't live up to their expectations of what a God-fearing Christian girl and well-mannered southern lady should be like. More often I did not.

Negative Scripts

When I talked about becoming a dancer, a singer, an actress, a writer, an English teacher, and going to college and traveling all over the world, Mama would say, "Sandy Lynn, you are getting above your raisin'!"

When I crawled too slowly down tobacco rows pulling weeds and suckers, didn't pick string beans fast enough, and couldn't focus long on shelling peas, Daddy would shout, "Sandy Lynn, you'll never amount to anything."

To top it off when I'd visit Grandpa at the country store, he would say, "You can't help from being ugly but you could stay at home." Other times he'd comment: "Come on in here and let me put a paper bag over your head...you'd look better that way." Not understanding his sense of humor, I thought I had to be "as ugly as a burnt mole" – a phrase often afforded to the most unattractive of the lot in our neck of the woods.

Casual comments from adults brought tears to my eyes but also motivated me to move mentally and physically beyond the limited viewpoints of a rural family. I decided that if I couldn't be "purrty" like my classmates Patricia, Elizabeth, and Jinger at Broadway School, I'd be smart so I read books, studied more, made high grades, excelled in extracurricular activities, and won awards.

As a child I suffered from low self-esteem because I didn't fit in on the farm and didn't know how to relate sometimes to even my best friends and caring teachers at Broadway School. Some of the negative comments from family motivated me to try even harder to impress other people.

Pond Saves My Sanity

Rumor has it that a man stopped at Grandpa's country store and asked if he could cut some timber off the land below our farmhouse on the family farm. In exchange he would create a pond so Grandpa and Daddy loved the idea.

As the trees came down and paths were cleared of limbs, a large opening emerged in the woods. The shift from tall trees and thick brush to a large hole that filled with water offered me a retreat away from home in the forest. I welcomed the baby fish that fattened daily and were so tame they would eat from my hand as I held the bread in the shallow water.

My sister Carolyn and I enjoyed feeding the fish and also the ducks and geese that visited there. My brother Jimmy sometimes swam there in an old inner tube. They did not understand my obsession with spending time at the pond and hiding in the woods. When I forgot about time and the sky grew dark Mama often screamed at the top of her lungs: "Sandy Lynn, get your butt home for supper. You are going to be the death of me."

My family certainly did not comprehend my need to be surrounded by Mother Nature and how Her soothing energy inspired me to write prose and poetry.

While I was a student in Josephine Gardner's ninth-grade English course, a senior from Campbell College (now University) in Buies Creek came to Broadway School as a practice teacher. One day he asked class members to write an essay about something meaningful. Naturally I thought about how the pond and the woods were my sanctuary.

I wrote this essay called Remembering:

"Through my childhood days there have been many depressing moments. There have been times when humanity has been very hard to bear. So, like many others, I have found a refuge…a place where wrath and tears are shed. Here, I am away from all people. I am away from the good people who would never harm me, and away from the bad people who constantly destroy the bright shore I have so boldly invented. I am away from the whole wayfaring world.

This place is none other than the woods. Here, Mother Nature embraces me in her loving arms. I truly love this world. No other place in the universe can bring me the satisfaction I receive here, and though this place can only be temporary, it is wonderful. I know that Mother Nature will never know how much I love her world; but yet I continue to surrender my mind and heart to her.

Though she is as naked as birth and as innocent as white, she knows my outside world and helps me through my heartaches like no human can do. She represents an oasis in my prevailing land of discontent. This oasis can never be conquered by anything or anyone, therefore I have assurance that there is always someone who watches over me."

The next day the teacher made an announcement that one student's essay was so well written that he intended to put it on display in a glass case at Campbell for college students to read. He said my name. Some students in the class clapped their hands.

That was the first time I actually realized that my passion for writing poetry and prose was a gift that might benefit others. I felt excited that someone had recognized my talent and encouraged me.

Creative Yearnings

As an oversensitive observant child I looked at life much more deeply than my peers, which sometimes led to a sense of separation from family and friends. I learned later that most artistic types feel this same aloneness and loneliness. When I experienced pleasure, my writing captured the sweet memories on paper. When I felt pain, writing soothed my soul and renewed my spirit.

Retreating often to Puzie's Pond I wrote from the depths of my soul. I also found tremendous comfort in Mother Nature. Writing and spending time with nature evolved as two activities necessary for my sanity, and that continues to be true.

While living on this isolated farm – certainly not close to the music and dancing lessons I craved – I could write. Grandpa's country store was always stocked with paper tablets and pencils.

Grandpa, Daddy and Mama couldn't comprehend a child who preferred reading, writing, singing, dancing, and dramatizing to working on the farm. For me, puttin' in tobacco and shelling peas left much to be desired as a way of life. I longed to follow the Muse speaking to me.

My special private place was the rusting-out blue and white '49 Chevrolet in our sunny backyard, certainly more inviting and often warmer than our old and cold farmhouse with cracks in the walls and on the floors.

Here I parlayed my interest in making up stories about my dolls into creating dramas about bold and beautiful people who lived in exciting places that seemed more interesting to me than participating in a farm family's simple life.

I Thought I Knew What Life Was

My performing studio was a secluded spot in the woods next to our seductive pond where I would sit for hours churning out my poetry and prose on paper. The pond's dam served as a suitable stage for my dramatic presentations – ranging from heavy-hearted monologues to humor-filled comedy acts. I sang and danced and bowed to my audience of fish, ducks, dogs and cats...my allies on my family's farm.

My family, my classmates, my neighbors...they laughed when I read my creations aloud. They howled for days when, at age 13, I told them I had written my first book titled *I Know What Life Is*.

While growing up and evolving into a teenager I wrote because I had to – tapping into my creativity was as important as pursuing academic studies and being involved in extracurricular activities. I bought diaries and composition books and filled them with poignant poetry and prose.

At school my favorite subject was English. I thought I had died and gone to heaven when I discovered Ralph Waldo Emerson and Henry David Thoreau who were involved with a movement called Transcendentalism in 19th-century America. They believed that it is possible to create a spiritual state through quiet meditation and by being one with nature. They considered material possessions and fame to be man-made desires, but preferred natural pleasures, including wandering through the woods and observing the pond through the seasons. In his famous book **Walden,** *Life in the Woods*, Thoreau stated: "Most men lead lives of quiet desperation and go to the grave with the song still in them."

With my unique philosophy of life and my overwhelming obsession with writing I felt like I heard the beat of a different drummer and was relieved that others thought and felt like I did…though no one in Buckhorn or Broadway!

Singing Off-Broadway

Writing was my soothing soul mate, but I loved singing tremendously. When I sang at churches and community events in the area and began to travel to places like Sanford, Carthage, and Siler City, I joked that I was singing "off-Broadway," even though most did not have a clue about what it meant. They had not read issues of *The New York Times* many hours at the main library in uptown Sanford or stayed awake nights thinking about musicals and cast parties that were taking place 600 miles away without me!

When I graduated from high school, second in my class, I carried with me an impressive list of achievements – president of the honor society, editor of the school newspaper, winner of the poetry award, and recipient of the American Legion countywide oratorical award. Despite all the teasing from other students who always thought I was strange they voted me Most Likely to Succeed during my senior year at Broadway High School.

While I didn't really know what life was I was determined to find out. I longed to write books and become rich and famous and marry an important man. We would have a huge house with rooms full of books – books I had written and books by great thinkers that I could read for hours without interruption. There'd be no one calling out in the middle of a poem: "Sandy Lynn, you get your butt home for supper."

Or I would become an actress, sharing my singing talent and dramatic ability on stages in theaters all over the world. I'd change my name to Alexandra or Cassandra because it would speak of sophistication and exude worldliness...besides, it would look better on marquees!

Lessons Learned

The things that cause us the most pain in life often prepare us to help others going through similar pain. People can hear us better when we've been where they are. These experiences allow us to bring hope to others. Empathy can only come from understanding.

Challenges with expressing my creativity and discovering who I really was encouraged me to work harder, dig deeper for gems, and be persistent in pursuit of my true self.

Through exploring our natural talents we become aware of what we truly love to do. Once we find our passion, it is our responsibility to cultivate it, keep tilling the soil, sharpening the saw, and honing our craft.

I discovered that by reading I could find other writers of like consciousness and I continued to research ideas.

Questions

Can you remember what you loved to do most as a child?

How did you overcome your obstacles with your family or with other people who did not understand or support your natural gifts?

Do you have an avocation that could actually turn into a money making activity and become a vocation?

Be yourself;
everyone else is already taken.

Oscar Wilde

But they that wait upon the Lord
shall renew their strength;
they shall mount up
they shall run, and not be weary;
and they shall walk, and not faint

Isaiah 40:31

6
Leaving Behind "Sandy Lynn"

Breech born with bronchitis on a cold day in February 1950 I struggled with health issues even as a baby. While I was growing in the womb my Mama was suffering with various illnesses, including continuous colds, anemia, and thyroid disease. Mama's ailments plus her medications affected my development as a person.

As a child I suffered constantly from long bouts of asthma and bronchitis. Daddy insisted I take a spoonful of honey every day for my lungs. When I was barking like a dog Aunt Gladys created a concoction of cough syrup consisting of 1/3 honey, 1/3 lemon juice and 1/3 whiskey and insisted I take a dose every few hours. However, home remedies were being replaced rapidly by modern medicine in our rural community.

Later I experienced painful menstrual periods and mood swings. dealt with emotional outbursts, mental confusion, and physical exhaustion. A conventional medical doctor who was treating my mother prescribed lots of antibiotics and Valium to relieve my many symptoms. Since Mama and Aunt Isabelle took Valium for their nerves the doctor automatically suggested it for me.

My writing kept me optimistic about the future. During my 12 years at Broadway School several teachers applauded my essays and term papers. In high school I edited the school newspaper *The Tattler* and wrote a regular column for *The Sanford Herald*, the hometown paper. After graduation I desperately wanted to go to college but my parents said they couldn't afford the cost.

For a while I handled secretarial duties at a textile company and for county offices which improved my typing skills and helped me understand more about how business and government functions. However, I lacked interest and heart for this work. Eventually I was hired as a full-time reporter at *The Sanford Herald* and discovered the power of journalism and its effect on the community. In this job I was expected to attend meetings, interview people, find stories, and I loved writing about diverse topics.

When the papers rolled off the press each afternoon I would go downstairs and eagerly pick up a copy and read through the pages. My hands would be covered with black ink, but my heart would be bursting with joy. I was a paid published writer!

The meaning of life is to find your gift. The purpose of life is to give it away.

At Christmas 1970 Ruby and Bud Lett celebrate at home with
Pete and Carolyn Lett McNeill, Sandy Lynn, Jimmy and Sharon Wood Lett
with their two sons, Billy and Wayne.
This picture was taken by photographer Jimmy Haire
when he and Sandy Lynn worked at *The Sanford Herald*.

We are indeed much more than what we eat,
but what we eat can nevertheless help us
to become much more than what we are.

As I see it,
every day you do one of two things:
build health or produce disease in yourself.

If this country is to survive,
the best-fed-nation myth
had better be recognized for what it is:
propaganda designed to produce wealth
but not health.

Adelle Davis, nutritionist,

Author of ***Let's Eat Right To Keep Fit;***
Let's Get Well; Let's Cook It Right;
and ***Let's Have Healthy Children***

Striving for Something More

During these 18 months as a journalist I knew there was no going back, I was born to report stories, however I felt like Eliza Doolittle and wanted to be *My Fair Lady*. I was a country bumpkin who was getting citified but I longed to go to college more than anything in the world. I focused on honing my writing skills, getting healthy, and saving money.

While seeking vitality in 1970 I read a popular health book **Let's Eat Right to Keep Fit** by Adelle Davis and began to take vitamin and mineral supplements. My first miracle happened when I discovered that taking calcium relieved menstrual cramps more than Midol ever could. I started taking B vitamins and noticed that my bouts of despair went away. I became interested in nutrition and began to focus on healing my body and my mind.

Davis was at the forefront of the whole foods movement in California and endorsed specific foods and various supplements to alleviate various symptoms. This nutritionist was one of the first to believe that additives, dyes, and preservatives in foods caused problems including depression, hyperactivity, and obesity. Davis was also the author of **Let's Get Well; Let's Cook It Right;** and **Let's Have Healthy Children**.

In my search for growth I became friends with another reporter who was old enough to be my mother, Margrette Stone who had an extensive background in the arts. She shared many stories from her diverse career and offered tremendous insights on different types of religions and spiritual ideologies. Her initials were MS so I called her Mysterious Sage. I felt like Margrette was the first person to ever really understand me, and she encouraged me to go to college because "you need to know what other people know."

Margarette Stone

While writing articles on activities at Sandhills Community College in Pinehurst and Southern Pines area I treasured the small campus surrounded by acres of woods. I decided to start classes there and applied for a part-time job at the local newspaper and was hired to work with editor and publisher Sam Ragan, who was highly regarded as a creative writer as well as journalist and was named poet laureate of North Carolina.

As I left Broadway behind, I was determined to overcome Daddy's constant comment "You'll never amount to anything" and make my mark in the world of journalism. I wanted nothing to do with farming and that way of life, and I looked forward to exploring possibilities. Little did I know then that my lessons from the farm were the backbone for my habits of hard work, persistence, and accomplishment.

35 Years Ahead of Time

When I moved to a more urban area…considered a resort which attracted lots of wealthy people who played golf and enjoyed fine dining…located 35 miles from Broadway I transported 35 years ahead of time. I relished the stimulating conversations, intellectual pursuits, artistic offerings, and popular culture.

In college this little country girl thrived. The accolades continued…first female student government president, Phi Theta Kappa scholarship winner, campus newspaper editor, and most outstanding student award. I was even nominated for homecoming queen so I guess I wasn't "ugly as a burnt mole" after all.

While juggling classes, my work with the local newspaper and as campus publication, I took small roles in theater productions. However, I realized that I had to focus on developing myself as a writer and had to put my acting and singing talents on the back burner.

During college days I read the play *Pygmalion*, written by George Bernard Shaw in 1913 when he was 57 years old. The story focuses Elizabeth as a Cockney flower girl who takes speech lessons from professor Henry Higgins, a phonetics expert, so she can pass as a lady. The play became the musical *My Fair Lady* in 1956.

In the script Higgins says "If you can't appreciate what you've got, you'd better get what you can appreciate." In creating my life off-Broadway I focused on finding work that I appreciated with the idea of educating and entertaining others.

During my student days at Sandhills Community College I worked part-time as a reporter and society editor for *The Pilot*, the weekly newspaper in Southern Pines. I felt fortunate to spend time with the editor and publisher Samuel Talmadge Ragan who was named poet laureate for North Carolina in 1982. While spending time with such a role model I was motivated to develop my writing ability and inspire my readers.

As North Carolina's first secretary of the Department of Cultural Resources and first chairman of the North Carolina Arts Council, Sam Ragan helped make the arts accessible to a wider audience.

Sam Ragan
(1915 - 1996)

Sandhills Community College

S. G. A. OFFICERS

Steve Mooneyham, Parliamentarian; Sandy Lett, S.G.A. President; Jack Stultz, Vice President; Edie Tatum, Treasurer; Roger McKoy, Senator; Laura DiRienzo, Senator; Jeff Viall, Senator. Not pictured: Susan Parler, Secretary.

As a college freshman I fell in love with a college teacher...my Prince in Shinning Armor. Bill grew up in a home in Michigan where his father was a university professor and he was expected to obtain as many degrees as possible. He encouraged me in my studies and extracurricular activities. Bill said I was the best thing that ever happened to him and I felt the same way about him. When he wanted to get engaged I was on a tight budget so I suggested he buy me four rings...tires for my car!

Later I decided to transfer to the best journalism school in the state at UNC-Chapel Hill and applied for a scholarship. I researched the best ones available and discovered there was one distinguished journalism scholarship given to one junior and one senior so I vowed to win. After being chosen as a finalist and receiving $500 I went to campus for interviews with the dean, professors, and editors from newspapers. I performed well, and sure enough I was the only rising junior who received the award.

By now I had figured out that I was ordained to be a writer, and if I believed in myself and trusted God, doors would open. I was thriving and looking forward to more advanced studies and exciting adventures.

Sandra Lynn Lett
UNC-Chapel Hill
School of Journalism Class of 1976
Yearbook Picture

I have never thought of writing as hard work,
but I have worked hard to find a voice.
All writers do.
Sometimes we are successful,
often we are not.
But long before the first chapter is finished,
and often before the first chapter is started,
we search and search to find a voice.

John Grisham

Health Challenges and Answers

A bout with serious illness during my junior year was the first inkling that life might not play out as I had expected. This crisis led me to an unlady-like distrust of conventional doctors (mostly chauvinistic white males), who had always been held in high esteem by sickly Southern women, and an "unholy" distaste for modern medicine and its frightening side effects.

Doctors diagnosed me with uterine fibroid tumors and endometriosis, a rare disease back then, caused by a hormonal imbalance so I was prescribed massive dosages of hormones that led to horrible side effects. The medicine was worst than the disease!

After a hellish stay in the hospital, a dreadful drug therapy program, and devastating toxemia from experimental hormones I was forced to drop out of college. Later when back in school my extracurricular priorities shifted and I became editor of a campus feminist magazine called SHE. This traumatic health crisis paved the way for my soapbox years as a flaming feminist and eventually a crusading holistic health proponent.

My fiancé Bill told me about a student in his class Caroline who had experienced miraculous results at a holistic health center and scheduled a meeting for us. In May 1975 I sought solutions at Beechwold Clinic in Columbus, Ohio. On the first day I had diagnostic sessions with an osteopathic physician, a chiropractor, a nutritionist, a counselor, and other experts. Dr. Ernest Shearer, chief of staff, said my endometriosis was related to malfunctioning glands and weak organs that needed to be rebuilt with nutritious food and natural supplements. He prescribed vitamins, minerals, herbs, and homeopathic remedies.

Dr. Shearer noted: "All our modalities are wonderful, but the number one cure is rest. When the body sleeps healing increases dramatically."

The chief of staff also detected low blood sugar and suggested that I eat a high protein diet featuring lots of seeds, nuts, whole grains, and fresh vegetables. Since fruits were high in sugar I had to balance them with yogurt enhanced with protein powder, bone meal, and yeast. After following Dr. Shearer's advice, my health improved dramatically, and a new way of living opened up for me.

That clinic was 500 miles from home and at least 50 years ahead of modern medicine – it focused on "traditional" healing because its modalities were passed down through the generations. The philosophy was simple: food is medicine; live plants and dried herbs are healing; movement is crucial; massage, chiropractic, and osteopathy are necessary for balancing the body and mind; detoxification is important; and a good attitude is crucial.

While a senior at Carolina I spent my spring break at Beechwold Clinic in Columbus where Dr. Shearer and other practitioners treated my illnesses and provided tools for promoting wellness. Meanwhile, I had planned a Fourth of July wedding in 1976 in honor of our country's Bicentennial with Bill dressing as Uncle Sam and me as Lady Liberty but put romance on the back burner. While my friends were interviewing for jobs and excited about next steps I knew I still needed treatment and guidance to get completely well so back to the clinic for a summer of learning and healing. As it turned out I ended my engagement and had a date with destiny and stayed four years in Ohio.

Wholesome Eating

While working in the kitchen and guest house as an intern I became totally involved with preparing live foods and began to totally grasp the idea that nutritious nourishment to the human body was as necessary as gas for the car. I attended lectures and workshops on various aspects of healing body, mind, and spirit and learned more about the concept of treating and restoring the whole person often referred to as holistic healing.

During this time I experimented with vegetarianism, partly because I wondered if giving up meat and synthetic hormones could help my endocrine imbalances. By now I had discovered creative ways to use soy, especially in the form of textured soy protein (TSP) and tofu, and knew how to combine foods to get all the amino acids in protein. I combined brown rice and millet with beans, nuts, and seeds to increase protein in my diet.

Experts at Beechwold Clinic did not encourage vegetarianism because of my genetic weaknesses but I felt it was healthier and more spiritual not to eat meat. I took a whole foods cooking class from Julie Evans and focused on baking bread from whole grain flours, making desserts with honey or molasses instead of white sugar and combining various beans and grains to get enough protein while curtailing meat.

For a while I bought milk fresh from a dairy farm and made butter, cottage cheese, and yogurt at home. I purchased corn meal, freshly ground at a local mill, and whole grain flours from a health food store. I belonged to a back-to-nature group, and we proudly called ourselves "health food nuts." For several years I ate like a saint – not even one bite of any foods containing white sugar, white flour, or table salt. However, flesh is dumb and addictions are powerful so I've had to crash and burn a few times but have always found my way back to health through natural remedies.

From 1975 to 1996 I regularly traveled to Ohio to obtain life-changing healing services at Beechwold Clinic. After Dr. Shearer died I continued living in harmony with natural remedies but never found a healing center like the one he created. The vision of the Beechwold Clinic will always be my intention: to draw upon nature's resources and remedies for getting rid of disease and dis-ease and to promote wellness.

My deepest desire in life back then was to be healthy and wise...to let go of Eliza Doolittle's shortcomings and become *My Fair Lady* every moment of every day. I have never given up on being my best!

Lessons Learned

Experiences in my life motivated me to explore new possibilities. It is important to look for new options when you don't like the results someone else prescribed for you; being open to new ideas and willing to learn from non-conventional sources; and realizing sometimes your passions are wrapped up in your life challenges.

It seemed impossible for a long time that it would be possible to get a college degree due to costs but I received several scholarships and also worked part-time at jobs that provided funds and professional experiences.

If you want something enough and hold the vision, the way to attract it will be made clear. I discovered that God's will for my life was much better than I expected.

My growth through the years felt a lot like the cycles I experienced on the farm of sowing seeds, watching seedlings grow enough for cultivation, and expecting a harvest. I certainly figured out about the importance of getting rid of worms and suckers and adding the right kind of fertilizer in regard to food and people.

Questions

Are you willing to give up your old habits to pursue your passion and create a fulfilling life?

What vision are you holding that currently seems impossible to you?

Is there a simple first step you could take to improve your diet and take more control of your health?

7

Claiming AlexSandra the Great

While living in Yellow Springs, Ohio for four years from 1976 to 1980 I was constantly exposed to diverse life-changing ideas and strategies. During this time I wore my hair to my waist, relished buying Bohemian clothes and gaudy jewelry from thrift shops and consignment stores. I soaked up the world of "isms," adopted vegetarianism as a way of eating healthy, and was intrigued by socialism until I questioned if it might mean giving up my 1969 blue Camaro with a black vinyl roof!

I was surrounded by very intellectual people who were highly involved with vegetarianism and feminism, and some were committed to anti-materialism. I tried to reconcile my obsession with creativity and healing with my desire to make money and have nice things. By now I was discovering that the American way of life was clearly divided between the haves and the have-nots.

During this time I enjoyed living in different worlds…the hippie mentality in Yellow Springs, the healing community in Columbus, and my journalism job in Dayton where I worked as a reporter at a newspaper. I reviewed plays, I wrote articles on the arts and health, and I also honed reporting skills by covering news related to lifestyle, education, business, zoning, and regional planning.

I was blessed with lots of friends but my favorite was Ann Klosterman, a woman I interviewed because of her focus on growing and preparing nutritious foods and using natural remedies for healing. Ann was a registered nurse, and she and her husband Cy had 13 children. She chose to add me to her large family in 1976 so I would have place to call home in Ohio.

"Mother Ann" Klosterman and husband Cy

Fondly I called her "Mother Ann," and she was a role model for demonstrating how a woman could be totally devoted to her kids and yet committed to constantly studying about body, mind, and spirit. She and Cy offered classes in their home. While gathering news I would stop at her house to eat lunch or take a nap to recharge.

While folks called me Sandy here I still longed for a more exciting name. I told my friend Theodora that I loved her name and her talents. She was an artist whose designs were used to create bold fabrics for clothes. When coming to visit me one day she ran into the house and asked for a piece of paper saying "I've had a vision…I saw your name in the sky." She wrote my name Sandra and then in front of it she wrote Alex and when I looked at AlexSandra I knew I had the perfect name for me. Cold chills came all over me. She and I laughed and jumped up and down like teenage girls at a slumber party. We both knew the deep significance of changing one's name.

Moving to Sanford

In summer 1980 I visited with my parents for a while and spent time with a dear friend Margrette who was diagnosed with cancer. My desire to help with Margrette's healing regime and an offer to become lifestyles editor of *The Sanford Herald* brought me back to Lee County for several years.

I continued my "health food nut" tendencies and helped friend Margrette determine healing aids to combat her cancer. She and I researched constantly and experimented with food as medicine. I bought 25-pound bags of organic carrots so we could make juice and drank it every day. We ate lots of raw food, including the alfalfa sprouts and wheat grass we grew. Fortunately Margrette's cancer went into remission, and our bond as soul sisters flourished.

As I attended many luncheons and banquets I adopted the adage "when in Rome" and began to eat meat again. I wanted to create balance in my life. When I started consuming sweets again I became addicted and figured out that flesh is dumb when it comes to eating habits. Mama cooked big Sunday dinners so I often indulged in too many rich desserts. On Monday morning I awoke feeling terrible and would take a nap in the afternoon before I could produce the weekly Food section. Obviously I did not always practice what I preached!

During the time from 1980 to 1987 I pursued my passions and was blessed with a paid position at a publication where I could express my creativity and start new projects like a health column, and weekly food section and arts sections. As lifestyles editor I loved going to work and being involved in the area. I lived in a house down a long lane surrounded by nature only a mile from the office so I could go home and eat lunch and take a nap before attending an event or going back to a quiet building. I took time to take walks either before going to the office or in the late afternoon. I learned that nutritious snacks and movement breaks allowed me to be more energetic and productive. Sometimes I arrived at the office at 6 a.m. to write major features before the hustle and bustle of breaking stories and tight deadlines took over the newsroom.

My life was not all work. In November 1981 I interviewed a new attorney in town David because he was acting in a play offered by the local theater group. We became fast friends. In my position I received free tickets to lots of events included plays, musicals, concerts, restaurant openings, etc. so we hit the road. David and I even agreed to be cast as Frank Burns and Margaret "Hot Lips" Houlihan in the local theater production of M*A*S*H. The drama was based on the 1969 novel and the TV situation comedy developed by Larry Gelbart that was broadcast from 1972 to 1983.

"Natural Living" Column

Since I was so enthusiastic about my experiences with healing I started writing a weekly health column called Natural Living, which was highly praised by readers and often scorned by mainstream medical practitioners. I advocated taking more personal responsibility for our health and suggested that people eat more nutritiously, exercise more regularly, and educate themselves about natural remedies to relieve symptoms and promote wellness. My goal was to share my experiences, research, and knowledge with the everyday person who was interested in feeling better and becoming healthier.

Here is my first Natural Living column published in March 1982.

"A new trend toward natural living emerged in the 1960s and 1970s and continues to permeate every area of our society. This interest reveals itself in the renewed emphasis on gardens and fresh foods; it shows up in our clothing as fashion designers return to cotton and pure silk; and it creeps into our homes with heating alternatives like solar energy.

"This concern is most apparent in the awareness of our diets as more people choose natural foods and avoid less nutritious substances. Even the most conservative segments of society are curtailing their intake of sweets and red meat and exchanging tranquilizers and pain pills for vitamin and mineral supplements. Health food advocates claim that many of our foods are processed to the point of being useless and in many cases can be harmful to our minds and bodies.

"Many natural living proponents believe that part of our health problems are caused by the artificial fabrics we wear and the many chemicals used in processing them. Some maintain that our sterile air-conditioned, centrally-heated houses with all their conveniences may be energy-efficient but rob us of our energy because of our lack of the fresh air and other aspects of nature.

"Natural living indicates a movement back to the basics – not an attempt to replace modern day convenience with primitive foods and methods, but a renewed appreciation of some customs and traditions that still have validity. We are living in a period of great discovery, but in our excitement, perhaps we have been too anxious to try the new and discard the old without proof that the new is better. While many medical discoveries are very beneficial, there are also side effects that can bring about negative results in the long run.

"As individuals, we must take responsibility for our diet, our health, our careers, our lives – and weigh carefully every factor before believing what we read and hear, and thus act intelligently upon these concerns. We must understand that every facet of our society is ruled by a complexity of political, economic, social, professional, and personal motives. We have naively believed that we are being taken care of by our politicians, our employers, our doctors without accepting the challenge of learning to look out for ourselves. While a delegation of power and division of labor are necessary, we must not forget personal obligations or sacrifice our right to decide what is best for us.

"What can one person do? You can start by taking control of your life by being informed – read, study, learn, experiment, discover what is best for you, whether it is the food you eat or the church you attend or the work you do.

"Only when each individual realizes that each spoke of the wheel must carry the burden in order for the machine to run smoothly can we experience personal success. And we cannot expect any system to satisfy us until we define our needs and seek to know who we are and what we want.

"In a sense the challenge begins with the food we eat, the thoughts we think, the lifestyles we choose. The new health advocates are indicative of the people who have taken personal responsibility for themselves and questioned the dictates of societal norms.

"They dare to ask.

"Why do we separate the bran and wheat germ in the flour from the white?

"Why do we use so many additives in our foods?

"Why do we wear synthetic fibers when nature provides us with its own?

"Why don't we construct our houses so nature can help them stay warm in winter and cool in summer?

"There are numerous questions, and there are answers that seem to change day to day, but there are basic principles that will always be true. So natural living is, in essence, an understanding of the importance of focusing on the natural in every area of our lives.

"Natural living is an approach towards evaluating the junk foods and the artificial things in every aspect of society. Natural living is a trend toward learning more about what is real, what is true, and what can offer us lasting value."

Book Becomes Business

Creating a new column every week I merged writing, health, and spirituality. Popularity of the column led to the publication of my first book, *"Natural Living: From Stress to Rest,"* in 1984. I enjoyed exciting adventures towards enhancing wellness, never taking prescription drugs and exploring natural solutions. I continued to be treated by various alternative practitioners trained to implement integrative approaches to preventing illness and improving health. I guess I became a prophet in my own country because I got lots of calls and comments from readers who had benefitted from my ideas and were implementing strategies to feel better.

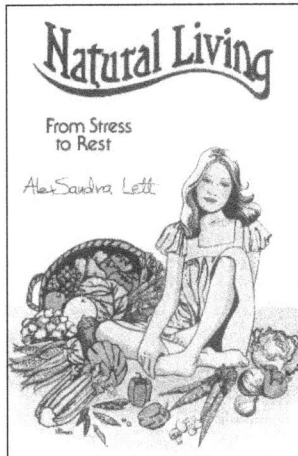

While continuing to thrive in my demanding job as lifestyles editor I offered programs on writing and working in the media, but my most popular topic was natural remedies and holistic healing. As word spread about my book invitations to speak to audiences increased so I offered programs and sold books.

I named my venture ALL Enterprises because of my name AlexSandra L. Lett and started learning more about what it means to own a business. A Small Business Center opened at Central Carolina Community College in Sanford and I signed up for classes, seminars, and workshops. I started attending events in the community sponsored by the college, the Chamber of Commerce, and professional organizations and began to understand the term networking to make personal and professional contacts.

The name AlexSandra Lett became synonymous with expertise in health but an offer to edit a publication in Charlotte inspired me to resign from my position as lifestyles editor and quit writing my column. When problems developed with the proposed job and I did not leave town I had already recruited someone else to take my position. As I produced my last articles and completed the last editions of lifestyles, arts, and food section I sat at my desk in the building alone that night. I was devastated as I left behind the only position I had ever held where I couldn't wait to go to work in the morning and where I felt like I had such a positive impact on the community.

I experienced the dark night of the soul as I waited for my next assignment where I could express myself and make a difference. I knew there was more to be healed and more to be revealed…and only my belief in my talents and faith in God could get me through.

Lessons Learned

When we've learned to integrate our natural skills and talents, while enhancing and honing them to new levels, we are often blessed with the perfect work situation to enjoy the fruits of our labor. The challenge is to recognize when our celebration is complete, and we are being called to the next higher spiritual growth level.

God often nudges us and we find ourselves being forced into new territory. Even though I panicked when I became unemployed some new doors opened for me to become co-creator of the next stage of my life.

Everyone has greatness in them. People need to allow themselves time to pursue a passion that will allow them to feel a greater sense of purpose for their lives.

Questions

What topic excites you enough that you love learning about it and sharing your experiences and insights with others?

What techniques do you use to impart knowledge to your family, community and/or business associates?

What achievements have you experienced that allowed you to celebrate your accomplishments?

What knowledge have you acquired that you would enjoy sharing with others?

8
Seeking Fame and Fortune

My **Natural Living** moment of fame faded away, but I continued to champion other causes and to search for answers to life's complexities. My exciting years as a lifestyles editor were replaced by confusion about finding different ways to use my gifts.

Even though I had learned a lot about starting a business, I didn't have the calling, confidence, motivation, or funds to become an entrepreneur. As it turns out a job opened up for me to do public relations for a travel agency that provided me a chance to see the sights way beyond Buckhorn, way past Broadway and Sanford, including a trip to Japan.

In 1988 I accepted a challenging position offering opportunities to develop my communication talents and learn new skills with North Carolina Public Television so I moved to Chapel Hill. For two years I was assistant editor for the monthly TV guide, prepared promotional packages about programs we produced in our state and for national PBS offerings, set up special events to launch new shows, attended various meetings, and honed my skills in public relations and marketing.

An unexpected offer to become managing editor of a new publication in Research Triangle Park took me into a different arena where my focus was reporting on big business especially large corporations expanding in the area. While learning advanced technology was difficult, I loved the creativity of writing and editing articles and working with a staff to sell advertising, design the publication, and distribute it in the Raleigh-Durham-Chapel Hill area. However, there was tremendous disharmony in that business and negativity with the owner. I asked God for a sign about what to do and sure enough, I got it – I was fired!

When a door closes a window opens. Realizing that I didn't really like punching a time card and working with people day in and day out I decided not to look for another job. Like most folks I was terrified of not drawing a paycheck but decided to bet on my talent and focus on writing.

Insanity is doing the same thing over and over again and expecting different results.

Albert Einstein

Starting a Business

So I started freelance writing from my home and sold articles to local newspapers and magazines. However, paying the bills was challenging. After researching and writing a book on the lifestyle of the Triangle – Raleigh, Durham, and Chapel Hill – for the Greater Raleigh Chamber of Commerce, I realized I could make more money researching and creating marketing materials.

I joined the Chamber and established myself as president of a public relations and professional speaking company. I named it ALL Communications to capitalize on my initials and I became all things to all people. When attending meetings and networking events I wrote the words AlexSandra the Great on my name tags. For better or worse, people remembered me!

My ego convinced me I was great. I became a cunning cat who could charm a snake out of a tree...and a tiger in the business world who longed for fame and   fortune. I wanted so much to prove my family wrong and be a smashing success.

While attending the Unity Church of Raleigh I met Judy Fourie, and we became instant soul sisters, connecting spiritually and hanging out socially. She owned an insurance agency and was very involved in the business community and encouraged me to network to get clients. She invited me to the Raleigh chapter of NAWBO (National Association of Women Business Owners).

Through NAWBO I met fabulous females who owned successful enterprises and I was inspired by Carolyn who loved growing plants and now serviced major hotels, Darleen who started selling typewriters at a young age and then used her business savvy to become a large computer services company; Sheila who began an advertising agency in mid-life and became a leader in her field; and Lana who left a secure position to start a company creating exhibits for trade shows. If these women could do it so could I!

Eventually I served on the NAWBO board and helped with booking speakers and promoting the organization. As I became part of this tribe, I was hired by other women business owners to help them promote their companies. Through involvement with the Chamber and other organizations I attended networking events and secured clients. I was on a roll and continued to increase my hourly fees.

Meanwhile I was speaking to diverse audiences about a wide range of topics, including strategies for marketing and getting media attention, ideas for releasing stress and promoting energy, and implementing steps to success. Audiences included executive women's luncheons, company enrichment programs, awards banquets, and small business centers at colleges.

*A big shot is a little shot
that keeps shooting.*

Becoming a Big Shot

During this time I was reminded of a comment my Uncle Gilbert said to me: "A big shot is a little shot that keeps shooting." I became well-known and relished the attention from people who viewed me as successful. Folks would even ask me to go to lunch and offer to pay for my meal and my time to brainstorm with them. I served on various committees and boards and loved spending time with wealthy friends, prestigious clients, small business owners, and high level executives.

My appearance reflected my reputation as a unique communications expert. I relished jewelry featuring fancy felines. Friends, fans and clients contributed to my impressive collection, ranging from five-inch broaches with diamond-eyed cats to rhinestone-filled pendants that accented my big bosom. I wouldn't be caught dead in anything that wasn't flashy red, bold blue, hot pink, bright purple, or jet black. Subtlety was not my strong point. I liked being referred to as a dramatic dresser and a charismatic creature. I had become an actress after all!

Finally I was away from the quaint little town of Broadway, living way, way-off Broadway in an area that thrived off diversity and intellect and claimed more PhD's than any place in the United States. Here I could strut my stuff and make big bucks. I became top tiger in a jungle that focused on succeeding due to smarts and aggression and achieving worldly success because of what I had learned and who I knew.

Doing What You Love

For a while I thought I had it all figured out until an intrusive uneasy feeling in my gut indicated that something was wrong with how I was living and making a living. Personally and professionally I was happy enough but very unfulfilled and I didn't know why.

While attending lots of programs on different aspects of building a business, developing our strengths and managing our weaknesses, outsmarting the competition, and using our mind to attract wealth, I became disillusioned. When going to the Unity Church of Raleigh and hearing enlightened speakers discuss various aspects of discovering God's purpose for our lives I felt uneasy. My ego reconciled that I enjoyed my work and appreciated my status in the business community but my higher self felt this deep hunger for something more.

For several years I had reflected on the importance of discovering our calling so we can really enjoy our work and feel in harmony with our right livelihood. I define a calling as a hunger that must be fed, a thirst that must be quenched, a constant craving that urges one's heart to seek outlets to create something unique… "you-nique."

Vocation is the place
where our deep gladness
meets the world's deep need.

Frederick Beuchner

Once an individual has answered the call ... usually an avocation turned to a vocation...it is obviously better than some boring job that just pays the bills and can be much more satisfying than even a chosen career. If one really responds to a calling, life becomes a soulful journey of giving up the lies he/she has been told about his/her work in the world, taking risks, and making decisions that will radically change everything in his/her life. A person with a clear calling will allow passion to lead to right livelihood, and in turn inner riches will eventually attract sufficient funds for greater abundance.

I read a fabulous book **Do What You Love, The Money Will Follow**, subtitled *Discovering Your Right Livelihood*, written by Dr. Marsha Sinetar and first published in 1987. The author is an organizational psychologist who left behind a secure job and comfortable career for something more...to focus on writing and consulting. Her work is totally immersed in helping individuals become more self-aware and inspiring them to have the guts to make dramatic changes towards wholeness.

In **Do What You Love, The Money Will Follow**, Sinetar states, "To find in ourselves what makes life worth living is risky business, for it means that once we know we must seek it. It also means that without it life will be valueless."

I really felt my work was worthwhile. It involved helping clients by creating news releases, crafting features that enhanced name recognition, promoting them to media outlets so they showed up in newspapers, magazines, and on radio and television programs. While I performed these services well I wondered if you can be good at something but feel that your labor lacks meaning and purpose.

I worked on promotional projects for nationally known individuals, including Dr. Deepak Chopra, author of several best-selling health and success books; Anita Roddick, founder of The Body Shop; and Barbara Hemphill, creator of organizing books, workshops, and software. Reading their books rekindled my long-term goal to produce manuscripts that would appease my longing to create and to write something significant that would really make a difference in other people's lives.

In my heart of hearts I had never given up on my deepest dream of writing books. A constant longing for something more overshadowed the deposits in my bank account. A stirring in my soul shifted my consciousness to wanting more spirit in my business.

Finally I begged God to take over my life...to use my talents and skills to be of greater service. I didn't know then that if you ask God for deliverance from your old self you'd better be prepared for destruction of the ego and downfall of your old life like the caterpillar living in a cocoon before becoming a butterfly. I did not know I was signing up for the most frightening journey I had ever experienced...the creation of a new me, a different calling, an exciting assignment that I never expected...

Lessons Learned

A person can be successful without feeling happy and/or fulfilled.

When your soul is calling you to something more – it can become painful if you don't take the time to explore new possibilities for expression. And yet when you follow that calling you will experience lots of growing pains!

Reinvention requires shedding our "old skin" to make way for the peace, love, and joy, which is rightfully ours.

Questions

Have you ever felt there was "something more" you should be doing?

*To find in ourselves what makes
life worth living is risky business,
for it means that once we know
we must seek it.
It also means that without it
life will be valueless.*

Dr. Marsha Sinetar, author of
Do What You Love, The Money Will Follow

*The time
always comes
when the pain
to remain
a caterpillar
is greater than
the metamorphosis
to become
a butterfly.*

9

Going Crazy...Getting Sane

"Am I going crazy or getting sane?"

I asked myself this question many times in the mid-1990s when I doubted the materialistic choices I had made in the pursuit of worldly success. As president of a communications company, I coordinated all types of activities for promoting people and businesses in the marketplace. Through consultations, seminars, and workshops I suggested marketing strategies for attracting customers and increasing   revenue. As a motivational speaker at luncheons and banquets I supplied food for thought on how to create success.

Through my second company, also based in Raleigh, TRANSFORMATIONS, I offered programs on eating nutritiously, releasing stress, increasing energy, altering metabolism, losing weight, and thinking positively. I knew a lot about healing body, mind, and spirit and spoke to audiences about my extensive research and extraordinary experiences with vitamins, minerals, herbs, and natural remedies. But I did not feel healthy and happy.

Spirit in Business

In 1995 and 1996 overwhelming encounters with egotistical clients, a severe illness, and a raging hurricane, and intense frustrations with my significant other served as wake-up calls. These disturbing crises led me on an astonishing voyage into the depths of my soul.

During this mid-life reassessment I was offered a wonderful opportunity to serve on the board of Spirit in Business. The organization offered meetings featuring speakers who explored ideas about how to place spirit as a priority in our occupations and in every area of our lives. My experiences with this group inspired me to put spirit into my own business.

As I examined my life and career I wanted to create a closer connection with God and to do work that would uplift my spirit rather than boost my ego. I realized that EGO signified Edging God Out...my ego had convinced me that I was something special because I was earning big bucks and hanging out with wealthy and powerful people. However, I did not like my focus on making money to buy more stuff and to gain prestige. I wanted to use my knowledge and talents to transform people's lives but had to start by changing myself. I began to view my Work in the world with a capital letter. I believed Work should nourish my soul...Work should enhance every facet of my life.

For more than 20 years I had implemented holistic healing strategies. In 1998 I decided to explore what I called "Wholistic Work" that honored spirit as well as business and to share compelling ideas that would motivate people to re-examine modern-day definitions of success.

Writing about Reinvention

My longing for tremendous changes in my career and my yearning for total transformation in my life increased. I wrote about my revelations and epiphanies in a journal, and eventually a book title evolved: *Going Crazy...Getting Sane*. The proposed manuscript would dare readers to reconsider the conventional approaches to earning an income in this money-oriented society and would inspire them to seek more meaning and purpose in their work.

To respond to my inner promptings about writing the book I needed to have faith in myself and in God and be willing to give up my old way of making a living. As I released clients I did not know if I was going totally out of orbit or if I was finally getting in control of my life. My business associates and even some close friends thought I was confused and compulsive but I courageously sought sanity and serenity through creative self-expression.

I responded "yes" to the calling that stirred deep inside me and began to totally trust God to direct my unpredictable journey to creative expression. Instead of focusing on achieving my self-centered goals and being attached to my self-imposed outcomes, I started seeking guidance for God's will to manifest. I had to let go and let God. Only God knew how I could best serve others.

And thus began an exciting expedition to find my distinctive voice as an imaginative writer, to discover my innovative approach as an inspirational speaker, to realize my unique purpose as a spiritual person, and to fulfill my divine destiny on planet Earth.

Hearing a Different Drummer

For many years I had felt what writer and philosopher Henry David Thoreau called "quiet desperation" until in 1998 the restlessness became a loud roar that forced me to look deep within myself. Thoreau is best known for his book *Walden*, subtitled *Life in the Woods*.

In *Walden*, while encouraging humanity to be true to themselves, Thoreau said, "If a man does not keep pace with his companions, perhaps it is because he hears a different drummer. Let him step to the music which he hears, however measured or far away."

Like Thoreau I felt overwhelmed by all the "shoulds" in society. I was tired of listening to all the voices that said I should be satisfied when I knew I was not developing my creativity, not living up to my potential, and not contributing my best to the world.

When discussing my frustrations with my favorite uncle Gilbert, founder of a building supply company in Sanford, we agreed it was time for me to start over and focus on free-lance writing. He suggested I move back to the area we both grew up in and build a house on family land. We decided on Lett's Landing, the site where my ancestors from Ireland had claimed 3,000 acres in 1745. Several Letts still owned part of the land, and Uncle Gilbert had a small cabin next to the Cape Fear River. Nearby we could construct my two-story house overlooking the river.

As I was leaving Gilbert's office that day I put a taped sermon in my car's cassette player, and it turned out to be about the prodigal son coming home. This seemed to be a sign from God! I excitedly believed that the grass would be greener in the country, far away from the city.

Prodigal Daughter

While starting construction on my house and in transition from Raleigh to Sanford I decided to temporarily rent a local residence. I found a remote cabin next to a large pond on a 50-acre farm. I had to pass over two cattle crossings and maneuver around some cows to get to my home deep in the woods.

Meanwhile my Daddy went visiting at the Cape Fear River and had a "hissy-fit" about his single daughter building a house in such an isolated area. There were locked gates at the two entrances to Lett's Landing but no one could control the folks who docked at the river to fish or folks often trespassed on the property to hunt. Daddy and Mama feared for my safety, so Uncle Gilbert was forced to cancel the construction project. At first I was very upset about the loss of my dream home, but I loved living in my cozy cabin in the woods with my computer in front of windows offering an incredible view of the water I named Paradise Pond.

Remembering the inspiration from Puzie's Pond from my childhood, now I had the opportunity to live by a pond and create my own utopia. After all, my soul brother Thoreau had left conventional society in mid-19th century New England and lived in a cabin on Walden Pond where he was determined to get in touch with what really mattered to him. Now in 1998 I wanted to hide out in the wilds of rural North Carolina and discover for myself life's secrets.

Re-creating the Thoreau experience, I welcomed the solitude and understood why I needed to tune out the voices of the world. Through my intentional connection with my heart and my constant communion with Mother Nature I found a sense of satisfaction and embraced a pervasiveness of peace that I had never experienced before. Like Thoreau and many others I listened to a different drummer, and finally I stepped to the music that I heard inside me...

AlexSandra Lett relaxes in the woods near the cabin
and always finds inspiration from Mother Nature.

This is one view of Paradise Pond where AlexSandra sought refuge
to find her voice as a writer.

From Avocation to Vocation

Many inspiring authors, motivational speakers, spiritual leaders, artistic types, and business futurists have claimed that if we do what we love, the money will follow. However, most people have discovered that this exciting concept does not always live up to its promise.

In using my natural writing ability and being true to myself to create a fulfilling career I realized the tremendous time, energy, discipline, and even pain required for personal and professional gain. I had risked everything to find my true voice as a writer. Inspired by various follow-your-bliss authors and speakers I decided there were crucial steps to move my writing avocation to a vocation that earned income to pay the bills as well as feed my soul.

What are the approaches necessary to move forward on the do-what-you-love-money-will-follow path? I knew the first strategies included:

(1) Honor our callings and listen to our heart's promptings;
(2) Experiment with our skills and abilities to discover what our gifts really are...activity is always better than analysis;
(3) Focus on developing our talents and determining which ones are ready to be utilized now...expect Divine Timing;
(4) Hone our craft consistently even when receiving no payment.

Digging Deeper

As I talked to others who longed to pursue their passions, I realized that people had different approaches to moving forward. Some of my friends thought if they could pray, meditate, burn incense, surrender to the Universe, do yoga postures, say affirmations, and take workshops, they would be automatically rewarded by manifestation of their wants. Many were not focusing enough on actually doing the work…some were so heavenly they were no earthly good!

On the other hand I had friends who thought if they worked enough hours, if they attended enough networking events, if they joined enough professional organizations, they could become enough.

Enough what?

In my rebellion I kept digging deeper inside myself for answers that spoke to my soul. While living in the cabin I wrote about 10 hours every day, read lots of articles and books, took long walks, and brainstormed with close companions. I felt more fulfilled than ever before as I wrote more chapters of *Going Crazy…Getting Sane*. The book was about inner revelation and outer revolution, and it was a unique approach to redefining success and discovering life's meaning.

I watched talk show hosts Oprah Winfrey and Charlie Rose interview many guests who spoke of finding their passion and purpose. I saw the sparkle in people's eyes as they talked about following their hearts, doing what they loved, and living in congruence with their life's purpose.

Missing Steps

During this time I was asked to speak for Spiritual Frontiers Fellowship, an organization that had been meeting monthly for several decades in Raleigh. I offered this topic: "The Missing Steps in Doing What You Love and Making Money Too." By the time I presented the program I knew what the additional steps were…to be persistent and create excellence.

So the missing steps that most people do not take are:

(5) Never give up on pursuing your deepest dream;
(6) Bring your work to a level of excellence that will lead to satisfaction for you and enjoyment to others who will be willing to pay for your extraordinary products and/or services.

These approaches can turn a passionate avocation into an exciting vocation.

Much to my surprise, as I continued to respond to my calling I was given and unexpected assignment to write nastalgia, Who would have thunk it?

As I do what I love and encourage others to do so I believe with all my heart that the money will follow, not always quickly but eventually, because we will reap what we sow. If we are steadfast in our love and our labor we will feel rich spiritually and ultimately reap the economic rewards of our vision and our work. We can expect the harvest!

Lessons Learned

While living in congruence with my view of Wholistic Work I gained insights about these themes:

* Choosing meaning over materialism
* Exploring the path to authenticity
* Drawing upon creative expression for therapy, healing and passion
* Learning to listen to the heart as well as the head;
* Living with intention instead of obsessing about specific goals
* Seeking true fulfillment instead of superficial success;
* Feeling in harmony with nature and appreciating its beauty and its glory
* Fncorporating spirituality in our work environment and bringing the sacred to our everyday lives
* Making peace with the past, and forgiving, loving and accepting ourselves, our families and others
* Understanding the craziness that can occur when shifting gears and changing consciousness – moving from emotional crisis to spiritual emergence

Questions

How are you feeling about your job or your work in the world?

Are you focusing on making money instead of nourishing your spirit?

Is your EGO encouraging you to Edge God Out instead of following divine guidance and pursuing your highest purpose?

The sun rising over the pond was one of AlexSandra's favorite experiences
during the four years she lived in a remote cabin.

10
Finding My Voice

Day after day, week after week I focused on expressing my talents and honoring my true self. Every day I wrote to my heart's content, prayed, meditated, sat in the swing by Paradise Pond, and took walks in nearby neighborhoods and in the woods. Many times I watched the sun rise over the pond from the windows in front of my computer. Often I gazed at the sun while it slowly disappeared below the trees. The constant creativity and soothing solitude combined with consistent communion with Mother Nature consoled my spirit and healed my heart.

For months I concentrated on writing the first draft of the manuscript *Going Crazy...Getting Sane*, subtitled *A Stormy Search for My Sacred Self*, which was a very deep story about the transformation of my Work and the metamorphosis of my life. This book revealed my powerful pilgrimage in search of peace and purpose and in pursuit of meaning and mission.

With my total commitment to writing I had come back to my deep desire from childhood to express my greatest gift and to pursue my purest passion. I loved composing on the computer more than any other activity and knew that somehow, someday I would make a living as a creative writer. For now I was working joyfully and feeling more in touch with my soul's purpose than ever before.

During these glorious months I also started writing poetry again, and the verses effortlessly flowed through me. Here is a poem about choosing to focus on writing:

WAY OF THE WRITER

There is a price to pay
for being a writer in this world.
In this calling I have no choice...
the way of the writer beckons me.
When my thirst is unquenched
writing pours in my cup.
When my hunger is overwhelming
writing fills my plate.
When the pain appears greater than the pleasure
writing feeds my spirit.
When the question looms larger than the answer
writing soothes my soul.

When my life is hell on earth
writing soars me into heaven.
When there is nothing to live for
writing gives me purpose.
When people pull me down
writing lifts me up.
When society makes no sense
writing offers me an answer.
When this universe seems tedious
writing brings unique verses.
When there is no song on my lips
writing brings forth magical music.
When I feel separate and apart
writing reveals miraculous melodies.
Words, sentences, paragraphs,
pages of poetry and prose...
they sing sweet phrases
they herald in my heart.

When Nothingness is large
and Somethingness is small
I seek the Mistress of Ministry,
I bow reverently to Her Wisdom,
I wed the Lord of Language,
I pay homage to His Words.
These are my Master Weavers
spinning yarns of love and light.
I grab their threads of truth
allowing them to unravel
taking me to a queen's gown
which I wear as I reign…
Leader of a courageous kingdom,
Landlord of a powerful palace,
Soldier in a sacred space,
Ruler of my divine destiny.
I hear the call of the Creator
I follow the canon of the Craftsman
I respond to the mystery of the Muse
I accept the mission of the Messenger
I choose the way of the writer

The cabin featured windows overlooking the pond so AlexSandra
set up her computer here where she could enjoy Mother Nature.

It Takes a Community

When growing up in Buckhorn community we kin belonged to an extended family – we socialized often with the Howards, the Griffins, the Boggs, the Carters, the Womacks. Throughout the year we shared fruits, vegetables, meat, milk, and other products from our respective farms with each other. When priming, looping, and curing tobacco leaves each summer we bartered with neighbors and worked as a team to bring in the harvest.

Meanwhile, at Broadway School mothers and fathers took turns picking up us young'uns after ball practice and cheerleading sessions and making sure we arrived on time at the ball games and got home afterwards. At Moore Union Christian Church my Mama and others served on various committees to keep activities running smoothly and also took turns cooking Sunday dinner for the preacher.

As I moved to diverse places I bonded with people who shared mutual interests. During college days I developed friendships with colleagues in classes and others who were involved in student government and extracurricular activities. I worked for various publications and formed bonds with staff members. I relished taking bread baking and   vegetarian cooking classes. We participants formed potluck groups to enjoy each other's health-oriented delights.

Since country folks back home did not appreciate my eclectic culinary offerings I donned the hat of professional photographer and took pictures at all family, church, and community gatherings and holiday celebrations. When I worked in Raleigh with prominent friends and clients I discovered that they loved my photography skills, especially when I put the pictures in albums as gifts. Through the years I realized that as a society we function better if we honor each other's strengths in our various undertakings.

Gifts from God

When I moved to the secluded cabin in the woods I discovered even more the importance of creating a supportive community. As I concentrated on finding my voice as a writer many soul sisters and blessed brothers offered assistance. Some read articles I wrote and made suggestions for improvement. As I honored my inner calling and trusted in God I rationed out the money I had to live on the next year. My rent and utilities were low and my needs were minimal but living with no income for months diminished my savings.

As I began to understand the term "starving artist" I attracted allies who fed me, including my landlord Joanna and neighbor Jinger. My long-term friend David dropped by each week with several cartons of freshly made foods from Mama Clegg's kitchen.

Through the months I felt fortunate to have such loyal friends who were there when I needed them the most. Several friends sent checks as gifts to support my creative efforts. Others recommended clients to me for personal counseling and marketing advice.

After about two years, my savings were depleted and I did not want to ask anyone for help. I had discovered a nature trail near the Rocky River and was walking in this area when I had what my Daddy would have called "a little talk with the Man upstairs." I reminded God that my finances were rocky and asked Him for guidance about what to do to earn some income while continuing to focus on writing. I determined that I needed $1,000 immediately and thanked God for its manifestation.

When I arrived home I talked to a new friend Judy who told me that one of her neighbors was executive director of an organization that was producing a major event but did not know how to proceed. I called the man that night and offered suggestions on doing a publicity campaign and a press conference in Charlotte, and he liked my ideas. I bravely stated that I required $100 an hour to provide those high-level communication services for this event that would take about 30 hours, and he agreed to hire me. I said I would draw up a contract and asked for $1,000 in advance, and we set a time in Raleigh to meet. This project led to several months of providing various types of marketing services and earning enough money to keep paying the bills. God answers prayers!

Writing Nostalgia

When rewriting another draft of *Going Crazy... Getting Sane* I continued to learn a lot about me, understand more about my childhood, and how my unhealthy choices in terms of personal and professional relationships had kept me from creating my ideal life. As I changed my consciousness the book's subtitle evolved to *An Awakening at Paradise Pond* to reflect how I was claiming my best as a writer and as a person...and yes, eventually, prosperity would come!

While writing the book I created many clever sales letters and an elaborate book proposal and submitted them to various publishers and literary agents. A helpful agent said she was impressed with my talent and my book but felt I needed to write something different. She commented: "You are a powerful Southern woman who had the guts to rebel against the status quo in order to find your true self. You need to be writing from that vantage point!" I did not have a clue how, but an unexpected opportunity to shift gears in my career developed.

One day in Spring 2000, I was taking a walk and thought about what I enjoyed on our farm was going across the road and listening to stories and hearing the news. Back at my computer I wrote some humorous anecdotes about Grandpa's country store and submitted an article to a newspaper near Carolina Beach. When it was published on April 7, 2000 I received lots of phone calls and e-mails asking for more. As stories flowed through me I established a weekly newspaper column in Wilmington and in Sanford and also published some articles in *The News & Observer* in Raleigh and in *Carolina Country* magazine. Editors and readers praised my columns and encouraged me to keep producing them.

I called my column "Lett's Set a Spell" because that was the way country folks pronounced sit. The first article, headlined Come on in, set a spell at Grandpa's country store, focused on Captain Puzie and Lett's Grocery and Filling Station. It started with this paragraph:

"Growing up on a huge farm in the middle of Nowhere – 12 long miles from a Somewhere called Sanford and 4 miles from a no-stoplight town known as Broadway – I learned early that Grandpa's country store was the social center of the Buckhorn community. On chilly days and nights local folks would hang out around Grandpa's potbellied stove to catch up on the latest gossip. On summer evenings farmers would set a spell outside and compare tobacco prices and crop yields while wives shelled peas for tomorrow's supper."

Ruby Turner Knight Lett and
Puzie Doyle "Bud" Lett pose for
a picture after getting married on
April 2, 1942 while Bud is
serving in World War II.
Later they became parents to
Jimmy Doyle, Mary Carolyn,
and Sandy Lynn. Their union
was one of the topics of
AlexSandra's columns.

For my column each week I recalled juicy gossip and
tall tales I had heard told often at the store: Mama and
Daddy getting married and him going off to World War
II; the first radio and television programs and how they
changed people's lives; the telephone party lines family
and neighbors shared. I explored a simpler way of
dating back to the time my Grandpa was born in 1888
near the Cape Fear River, then helped build Buckhorn
Dam in Verta Cox's back yard, married her and had nine
young'uns. Through the weeks I also shared stories and
reflections about growing up on the Lett farm in the
1950s and 60s.

As I wrote about generations of Letts and other
colorful characters I fell in love with these country folks
and relished their appealing anecdotes. I longed to
chronicle oral traditions and sweet memories from the
past. In this process I found a new voice as a writer, and
each week I continued to discover interesting stories to
share...enough yarns to keep me busy for a lifetime.

Emergence of Book

After I sent sample columns to an editor at a national publishing house who was reviewing my *Going Crazy ... Getting Sane* proposal, the editor became more excited about publishing a book tentatively titled Grandpa's Country Store. She discussed buying the publication rights and offering me an advance payment so I could focus on completing the book. However, I discovered it would take 18 months to turn the manuscript into a book via design and production and get it into the marketplace. By now I was getting constant calls from readers who wanted me to compile my columns into a book to give as presents for the upcoming holiday season.

As I researched self-publishing and talked to some companies who specialized in printing books I was about the next steps. On Labor Day Monday 2000 I was working on the manuscript and decided to ask God for a sign about what to do about printing some copies of the book now and later considering a national publisher.

About lunchtime the phone rang, and it was a man named Jim, the president and owner of a company in Hazlet, New Jersey who traveled often in the South and had been reading my articles. He complimented me on my humorous writing style and my entertaining story-telling ability. He said he would like to buy some books for Christmas presents, and when I told him I had been getting estimates on printing hard covers and paperbacks he insisted the books should be hardbacks because they were more suitable for gifts. He ordered 250 copies for clients and we decided on $22 each including postage. A few days later a check for $5,500 arrived and I needed $4,000 for my first payment to a printer. Yes, God had touched a man's heart in New Jersey to give me the message that I must publish the book now.

Friends pitched in to help me edit the book, and I
hired a graphic designer to create artwork and lay out
the pages and create the cover. Everywhere I went for
days I asked for people's input on the book title and
sent out numerous e-mails seeking advice. One of my
proposed titles was **Forever People in a Timeless Place**
because I felt like the folks I was writing about were
forever symbols of a way of life in the country and those
types would always be around. The country store was a
timeless place where people gathered to connect and did
not care about time.

Three different people suggested *A Timeless Place*
because it was easy to remember and captured a simpler
way of life when folks would set a spell and not care
about time. To tie in the name of my newspaper column
I chose the subtitle *Lett's Set a Spell at the Country Store*.
The emerging book revealed God's calling for my career
and I just followed the path of least resistance. As I
persisted in creating excellence in my work everything
fell into place for me to compile these columns into a
book that ultimately provided enough income so I
could keep writing.

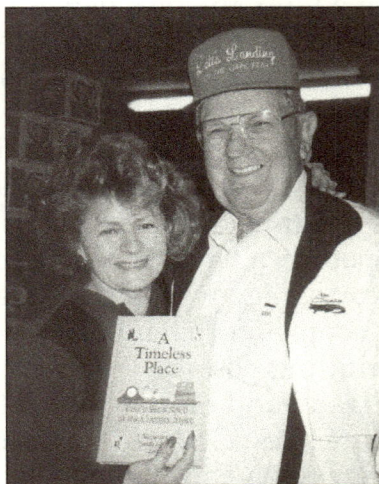

AlexSandra and her Uncle Gilbert
celebrate the 2000 edition
of her first nostalgia book.

A Timeless Place was launched in November 2000 at a big party at Lee Builder Mart, co-hosted by Gilbert, his son Tony and wife Rozie and daughter Janice and husband Art Coleman. Family, friends, and fans traveled for many miles to celebration the birth of my baby. Refreshments included sodas, Nabs, and MoonPies.

Capitalizing on the holiday sales season I proceeded to autograph copies at bookstores, gift shops, Christmas open houses and shows, and hawked them straight out of the trunk of my car. I was pleased to finally make money for my creative expression.

Unexpectedly I had found a unique voice as a nostalgia writer, and I was the author of a book that readers and customers were buying. I had followed the way of the writer and my career was going in an exciting direction. More importantly, I had discovered a greater purpose for my life.

My calling as an artist and my voice as a writer turned out to be the integration of all the pieces of my experiences…growing up on a farm, being exposed to entrepreneurs like my Grandpa and Uncle Gilbert, going to college and connecting with many types of people, working with newspapers, magazines, television, and radio, owning a company where I promoted people and products, and finally starting all over with a vision to express myself in the most creative and enjoyable way possible.

Finally I came home to my innate gifts and was sharing them for passion and profit….and isn't that the ultimate fulfillment?

Lessons Learned

By now I have figured out that a calling is not some mystical, magical thing that will show up and slap us in the face. As I followed my bliss and suffered a lot of blisters along the way I realized that nothing can take the place of persistence in the form of hard work and focus.

Life had come full circle. I ran from the farm even though the way of life there ended up being the roots for my calling...starting with being so frustrated with constant chores that I began to write by the pond. I wanted to be citified and discovered that I could actually earn a living and be successful in the arena of big business, budding entrepreneurs, and professional speaking. However, my love of creativity, exploration, and nature brought me to a higher calling.

To turn an idea into reality it takes support from the community, which may not look like anything you imagined.

Questions

Finding your voice often is tied to something you feel passionate about so is there something in your world that makes you feel extremely angry or sad?

How could you bring your passion into creating new solutions to problems in society?

What are you willing to sacrifice to find time to pursue your passion?

Think of examples in your life where you had the support of your community: family, friends, co-workers or whoever supported you physically, financially, mentally or emotionally. How did their support contribute to your short-term objectives and long-term goals?

11
Blooming in Buckhorn

The publication of a hardcover edition of my first nostalgia book *A Timeless Place*, *Lett's Set a Spell at the Country Store* shifted my career and changed my routine from a focus on writing to promoting. This book portrayed a simpler way of life through anecdotes, history, and humor and featured compelling photographs. It sold well to readers of my columns and new fans all over North Carolina.

Unexpected doors opened in terms of appearances that led to a broader exposure to all types of people. After hanging out with the big shots in the Raleigh area for several years, it was interesting to sell my books at events attended by many farmers and people who relished the modest life of my parents, grandparents, and ancestors in Buckhorn community.

Taking a grassroots approach to marketing, I autographed books at numerous community festivals, farmers markets, craft shows, antique emporiums, holiday markets, as well as conventional venues like gift shops and bookstores. With my trunk filled with product I hit the road like a gypsy for about 150 days that year and sold so many books I decided to create another edition in paperback in 2001 featuring more photographs.

The launch party at Grandpa's country store was scheduled the week that the twin towers in New York City were bombed, and the sense of security we had felt in the United States was destroyed. However, patriotism was high and love of family and tradition prevailed. As it turned out the launch served as a symbol of what was right in America and that included gathering with family, neighbors, and friends to celebrate the simplicity that created our nation and to cherish customs in every community. Ironic that such a horrible tragedy would skyrocket sales of both editions of *A Timeless Place* and also remind me that my work was meaningful.

AlexSandra relaxes at a book launch party
with Mama, Daddy, and her sister Carolyn.

AlexSandra socializes with her first cousin Tony Lett in front of
Grandpa's country store where the launch party was held
for the 2001 paperback edition of *A Timeless Place*.

Requests for programs offered me opportunities to speak to people of all ages at schools, churches, senior centers, and civic clubs as well as professional meetings. When preparing to perform in a talent show, I went through my closet for a costume and discovered that Aunt Isabelle had given me her 1968 Easter outfit…a thick yellow polyester frock featuring coral flowers and green leaves and a straw hat with coral flowers. I donned it with suntan hose and white pumps we women wore back then for providing a brief five-minute humorous program. The next day a meeting planner who had been in the audience called and hired me as the opening act for a multi-state convention.

And thus began a new way of relating to audiences through comedy that stimulated lots of laughter and opened my heart to providing more humor to people through my stories and experiences. Once in a while I even get dramatic and sing a happy tune.

As long as we are persistent
in our pursuit of our deepest destiny,
we will continue to grow.
We cannot choose the day or time
when we will fully bloom.
It happens in its own time.

Denis Waitley

AlexSandra poses in her Aunt Isabelle's
1968 Easter dress....yellow with coral flowers
and green leaves....while performing at a meeting.

AlexSandra the entertainer
dramatically shares stories.

The Homecoming

Writing stories about family and home made me appreciate and miss my rural roots. Like my ancestors, I wandered in the desert of exploration for a while, and like Moses, I stayed too long in the wilderness before I finally realized that "Lettsville" was the best place to live and grow. I felt led to go back to my home community to spend more time with my parents.

Since I was making money as a writer and speaker, and interest rates were low, it was a good time to purchase property. I prayed to God for the ideal place to call home. I told family and friends I would love to buy a house on a pond, and soon afterwards my friend Lois called to say her sister Diane and husband Johnny were going to move to the beach and would let me see the house first.

When I entered the circular driveway featuring a pond in the front yard I didn't really care what the house looked like on the inside – I was home. As I noticed the tall pines and thick hedges on the grounds and the woods and pastures nearby I savored this sacred space. Here I could enjoy the inspiration of Mother Nature, the quiet of country living, and privacy needed for creative explorations.

In terms of space I loved the large game room with a pool table where I could spread out my projects and set up my computer. My new office was bigger than the entire first floor of my cabin but it lacked large windows overlooking the pond, but my pond was nearby. Yes, I was the closest to heaven on earth I had ever been. Also I relished the separate three-car garage because finally I had room for old manuscripts, portfolio samples, and all the paraphernalia that comes from writing and publishing through the decades..

When I moved back to Buckhorn community in October 2002 I reestablished a deeper connection to the land, my family, and my heritage. Mama and Daddy were very glad that I moved so close to home. They were relieved that their gypsy child had finally settled down and were still hoping I would wed and experience a loving relationship like them.

While I loved living next to my new pond, I also welcomed the proximity to Puzie's Pond on the Lett farm. Mama and Daddy were in their 80's, had been married for 60-plus years, and were living happily in the same farmhouse only three miles down the road. I felt fortunate that I could set a spell with them often. I enjoyed residing close to other kinfolk and felt in the flow with my divine mission.

In 2002 AlexSandra buys a house on a pond
three miles from her home place in Buckhorn community.

Gilbert and Bud Lett, brothers and friends, stand tall at a family gathering
just before both developed serious health problems in 2004.

AlexSandra celebrates her mother's 80th birthday with her parents,
Bud and Ruby Lett, in 1999.

Green Pastures

During this time I wrote an article called *Coming Home to Green Pastures*. Here is an excerpt:

"My homecoming was divine justice – Grandpa and everyone teased me so much about being quar that I vowed to leave the Buckhorn-Broadway area forever, and here I was back home "eating my words.

"Even with Buckhorn's colorful characters and captivating gossip Grandpa found delight in regaling folks about his strange grandchild "Sandy Lynn" and her writing obsession. He was amused when I brought my paper tablet and freshly trimmed pencil to the country store to take notes for recording stories.

"Folks in Buckhorn, Broadway and beyond yakked about how "Sandy Lynn" moved every few years, traded in significant others like used cars, and changed jobs way too often. I confess I had an itch that always needed scratching – I soothed it by experiencing new friends, different places, and unique adventures, but I never found a lasting home. I lived in many houses, some spacious and expensive, but my restless spirit didn't find peace there. I always believed that the grass was greener on the other side of the fence.

I thank God that
my wandering spirit
rests easily now
in the fullness of my harvest.

"Every day I thank God for the Good Life, and especially to be living in the country and surrounded by cows and horses grazing in the fields. I am blessed with a wonderful family and caring friends. I peacefully look forward to more holidays rich in family traditions and community customs.

"Now I live in green pastures every day, and even as the grass turns brown, and the trees go bare, I understand there are seasons of the fields like the seasons of the heart, and all is well. I thank God that my wandering spirit rests easily now in the fullness of my harvest. I am grateful that I have returned to my roots, but more importantly that I have come home to the country girl with an open heart."

Joy and Sorrow

Since starting my Lett's Set a Spell column in 2000 I depended on various oldsters in the family for history and anecdotes, including Mama and Daddy and my cousins Nathan and Mary Alice Lett Crissman, Eula Lett Wilson, and Maxine Patterson. However, it was Uncle Gilbert who helped me the most. Sometimes I would visit him and Aunt Isabelle, and Gilbert and I would talk for hours, take a break from lunch, and then go back to talking a mile a minute. Aunt Isabelle would say, "You are two peas in a pod!"

When I settled back in Buckhorn Gilbert was disturbed that I was mowing my giant yard with a small push mower. He brought over a highboy lawn mower for me and took his riding mower off the trailer, and we joyfully worked together on the yard. This became a favorite get-together. Gilbert would pick up lunch and snacks for our breaks. Afterwards we would sit on my sun porch...he in the big white rocking chair and me in the swing, and we would share stories about family and friends.

Sometimes we would ride down to the land where our ancestors from Ireland had settled on the Cape Fear River in 1745 and originally owned about 3,000 acres. This was called Lett's Landing and became a well-known fishing spot located at the Lee-Harnett County line. This land will always be part of our family's heritage. By 2002 at least 300 acres remained in the Lett name, including the 180 Gilbert owned. He and I liked to sit on the back porch of his cabin where the river connected to the land, him talking constantly and me taking notes.

Responding to the needs of my fans I continued writing anecdotes and reflections in my weekly column and articles in other newspapers, magazines, and on websites. Eventually I published additional books, **Timeless Moons**, *Seasons of the Fields and Matters of the Heart* in 2004, and **Timeless Recipes and Remedies,** *Country Cooking, Customs, and Cures* in 2005. My business Southern Books & Talks was continuing to provide me with an ongoing sense of satisfaction that I was a published author who could actually make enough money to pay my bills!

Life was ripe for the pickin.' I did not know then that soon I would be sharing reflections about care-giving, dying, grieving, and healing…all seasons of the soul.

My zest for capturing humor and history changed to an obsession with writing about our family's crises as I recorded the declining health and constant care of Mama, Daddy, and Uncle Gilbert. Daddy died in 2003, Mama in 2004 and Gilbert in 2007, and life was never the same again. Without a husband and without children, I felt like an orphan, but rallied up to honor their passions, their lessons, their contributions in another book **Coming Home to my Country Heart**, *Timeless Reflections about Work, Family, Health, and Spirit*, dedicated to Uncle Gilbert in appreciation for his love of life and labor and published in 2007.

While still grieving I enjoyed dating several guys and returned to ballroom dancing classes to find joy in movement and social events. Soon afterwards, I fell in love, got engaged, and started planning a wedding with someone who looked very much like my father, but that's another story for another day.

Economic Challenges Force Innovation

What was it I said that every time I thought I had life figured out things shifted?

Being on the road 100 days a year autographing books was exhausting but marketing was just as important as writing in my profession. For eight years I depended on book sales for 80 percent of my income, and then in 2008 the economy in the United States crashed. When most buyers were afraid to purchase luxury items and even curtailed giving Christmas presents I felt the pinch in my pocketbook. When the holiday season did not prove lucrative as usual I had two choices: I could be upset and worry about finances or I expect the new possibilities that comes with every challenge.

During those financially trying times when lost jobs and diminished funds dominated the news it was natural to feel frustrated and even frightened. There was less money circulating, however I believed this could inspire motivation to be more creative, inventive, imaginative, artistic, resourceful, innovative, and ingenious. With every challenging crisis there is the exciting opportunity to change our lives. I decided to make some changes to my house, including upgrading all the floor coverings and refinancing to get a lower mortgage payment. I also shifted my physical structure by exercising more through walking and taking ballroom dancing classes.

For mental stimulation I enrolled in a weekly mastermind group meeting. The textbook was *Think and Grow Rich!*, written by Napoleon Hill and published in 1937 and perhaps the best-selling book on success. The class focused on positive thinking principles and attracted participants who are committed to living on a higher level of consciousness and supporting each other in achieving goals.

While improving myself physically and mentally I also renewed myself spiritually. I attended more church services, read more inspirational books, and drew upon encouraging from Bible verses. My favorite is from Isaiah 40:31: "But they that wait upon the Lord shall renew their strength; they shall mount up with wings as eagles; they shall run, and not be weary; and they shall walk, and not faint."

"Ok, God," I said "what next?" As usual I asked for a sign and I got it.

Creating Audio CD's

While being open to new opportunities for generating funds I received a phone call from Shawn L. Faircloth, volunteer coordinator at the N.C. Department of Cultural Resources' Library for the Blind and Physically Handicapped in Raleigh. She wanted to know why my nostalgia books were not available on audio and I told her it was too expensive. She offered free studio services if I would read my book, *A Timeless Place*. The Library would handle producing audio books for their customers, and I could duplicate copies to distribute to others.

In contacting several companies that duplicate and replicate CDs (compact discs) and DVDs (digital video discs) I learned about making my product "retail ready." I discovered that a guy named Bill Tripp had a million dollar studio for recording musicians plus a production department for duplicating and printing CDs and packaging them near Sanford.

Within a few days Bill had replicated four CDs from my master copies and packaged them in a professional case featuring the cover of my book. Now I had an audio available to customers who preferred to listen instead of read books. With a new CD set and four books in print I continued peddling products and making progress.

Onward and Upward

When I awoke on New Year's Day 2011 I felt like I had overcome the challenges related to economic crisis of 2008 that had affected most businesses. I was optimistic about the refocus of my life from writing and promoting books to speaking to audiences. As usual I vowed that this would be the best time of my life, however in recent years a fog began to take over my brain, and I struggled to remember things. Finally I decided to try something radical about changing my diet. Several of my friends were getting great results from looking at their food allergies and sensitivities and avoiding certain foods.

After eating bread I felt sleepy and noticed my stomach would swell like a balloon so I researched diets void of wheat and read a lot about the gluten-free culinary plans. Gluten is a protein found in grains such as wheat, barley and rye. Symptoms of gluten sensitivity are usually gastrointestinal problems such as bloating, flatulence, gas, and diarrhea, and other signs may include joint pain, exhaustion, and headaches. People who are allergic to wheat complain about fuzzy thinking and sometimes dizzy spells. While these symptoms may relate to gluten intolerance – commonly called celiac disease – they can occur with dozens of other ailments as well.

Sure enough, when I totally released gluten from my diet I felt dramatically better immediately, and my mental clarity and physical energy increased dramatically. Again, I was reminded that food is medicine!

Speaking on Reinvention

While I sometimes offered programs on releasing stress and healing body, mind, and spirit, people seemed to want to hear about reinvention. The audience and I had a wonderful time when I provided a humorous presentation "Going Crazy, Getting Sane" at a multi-state convention offered by Delta Kappa Gamma, a prestigious educational organization with membership comprised of teachers, principals, superintendents, and administrators. I felt like I was in alignment with my right livelihood.

After presenting a program for the American Business Women's Association (ABWA) in Raleigh on "Doing What You Love and Making Money Too" news spread, and I started speaking for other chapters in different towns and also for conferences.

Doors opened in terms of offering enrichment programs for ABWA and Delta Kappa Gamma throughout the state and in the southeastern United States. In turn this led to more invitations from different groups. After these programs I was also allowed to sell my products.

Within a few months I had created a name for myself as an expert on reinvention so the phone kept ringing. My audiences included executive women, businessmen, senior citizens groups, members of Chambers of Commerce, and attendees at big conventions throughout the state. I spoke at schools where I offered humorous stress relief programs for teachers and staff and also entertaining and educational programs for elementary and high school students. I even presented sermons for morning services at churches as well as speaking for women's luncheons and banquets where I shared stories about how God had connected me with the perfect people and ideal situations to create a unique career.

My program "Going Crazy...Getting Sane" was about my leaving behind my focus on fame and fortune to focus on discovering my authentic self. When taking risks people are more likely to be called crazy than innovative, however I believe we must go out on a limb to pick the best fruit. I inspired attendees to follow their bliss but also be realistic about experiencing some blisters in implementing steps to success. Getting sane involves being true to ourselves, expressing our talents, finding our purpose, working diligently, and feeling fully alive.

Drawing upon my experiences as a misunderstood little girl I created a new program "It's Never Too Late to Have a Happy Childhood." I offered insights on reframing situations...realizing that our families did the best they could as they provided us with opportunities to learn lessons. I also discussed making peace with our past, forgiving others, and feeling lively, excited, and passionate whatever our age. By thinking young, honoring experiences, and by implementing healthy living strategies people can feel totally alive. After all, it's never too late for any of us to decide to have a happy childhood! Also aging means growing older yet wiser and offers opportunities for pursuing new adventures in body, mind, and spirit.

Teaching My Truth

While enjoying my new focus on speaking I thought a lot about how many of the people in my audiences had asked questions about how to turn their avocations into vocations. I wondered how I could offer my insights on a more practical level.

How could I serve individuals and businesses and also stimulate my creativity and draw upon my knowledge and skills? What builds businesses?

What creates a community? The answer is the same: people helping people. I decided it was time to teach my truth and make a difference in my home community.

The Bible says it was hard for Jesus and others to be considered a prophet in one's own country, but I had certainly attracted lots of loyal readers for my weekly column in the local newspaper and I had sold a lot of books in the area.

With an attitude of nothing ventured, nothing gained, I contacted directors of the Small Business Center at Central Carolina Community College (CCCC), based in Sanford, about offering workshops to help people who needed encouragement as well as tools and techniques to overcome obstacles in the current vulnerable economy.

I wanted students at whatever age to understand the practical aspects of pursuing passion and taking their products and/or services to the marketplace. I outlined specific steps and strategies necessary for succeeding in business.

While speaking often on "Doing What You Love and Making Money Too" I added another workshop on "Marketing Your Products and Services." When starting a new venture or building a business, marketing products and/or services is a crucial component for budding entrepreneurs, small businesses, and large companies. The term marketing serves as the umbrella featuring spokes like advertising, promotion, publicity, public relations, media relations, event planning, strategic   partnering, networking, social media, etc. These tactics will establish a business in the marketplace, attract customers, stimulate sales, and help attain financial goals.

Meanwhile I learned about new ways of marketing, including social media. I signed up for workshops with Martin Brossman who collaborated with Anora McGaha to create a book titled *"Social Media for Business,"* and subtitled *"The Small Business Guide to Online Marketing."*

Through his seminars at numerous colleges Martin helps others understand the impact of using social media and shows attendees how to effectively incorporate tools on the web to make friends and influence people. In the introduction to his book Martin states: "Social media is where the conversations about you, your company and your products are taking place. Social media is where you build or lose the trust of your future customers."

As I learned social media I also started teaching the basics in my programs on marketing and entrepreneurship. Later I offered additional workshops on Getting Free Publicity in the Media and on the Internet, which included how to write a news release for publications and television and radio stations and how to post on online media outlets and other platforms; Tools for Thriving Professionally; and Publishing and Promoting for several community colleges.

When teaching principles to individuals and entrepreneurs as well as seasoned professionals I realized that we have an obligation to communicate our knowledge and experiences that will benefit others. As I traveled the state to motivate other audiences I did not pretend to be a prophet in any town. I was just sharing some insights I gained from suffering long, studying a lot, working hard, making tons of mistakes, and rising above circumstances.

While speaking to audiences about new topics I also altered my Lett's Set a Spell column to include ideas about how to experience greater satisfaction personally and more prosperity professionally. I must speak my truth!

Lessons Learned

I was amazed at the remarkable timing of the release of my book during the 9/11 tragedy, our nation's darkest hour, when people were longing to be reminded of a simpler time and family values. I was able to bring comfort to people who were hurting, and product sales provided me with money for the down payment of my house.

During this time I felt tremendous gratitude for moving to the ideal home, spending time with my family, being close to my parents and Uncle Gilbert during their dying days. I was amused at the ongoing synchronicity or Divine Timing of situations in my life…being led to the perfect place by the Creator so I could be of service to others.

While I continued to gather anecdotes and history from family members I honored my heritage more and relished providing education and entertainment to readers and audiences. Even my articles about dealing with caregiving and death were appreciated by others who told me that I gave language to their pain and offered soothing words during their many trials and eased their grief.

I came to believe even more in divine guidance. When we are following God's purpose for our life, we don't get to say when the blooming happens or when it's time to fully reap what we've sown. We have to trust and allow the Creator to guide us to our highest good.

I have always believed that when one door closes another opens so as book sales declined, speaking engagements increased therefore I had the opportunity to do more research and develop keynotes, seminars, and workshops.

Questions

What are you grateful for in your life?

Have you considered keeping a journal to remind you of all the good you have?

Are you being called to trust God in some area of your life?

Have you ever experienced divine guidance where something happened in the most perfect timing for you?

Have you noticed that while one phase of your life became challenging, another aspect was revealing new opportunities?

Over every mountain
there is a path,
although
it may not be seen
from the valley.

James Rogers

12

Intervention and Re-Creation

When I used to skip church or be late to the service on Sunday mornings a minister used to say to me "The closer you get to Heaven the harder the devil works." I was obsessed with reinventing my health and my business when Fate intervened on 11-22-2011.

However, eventually I figured out that God was leading me in a new direction. In **The Bible**, Romans 8:28: "And we know that all things work together for good to them that love God, to them who are the called according to His purpose."

The longer I live the more I believe in divine intervention. For me early signs for transformation begin slowly with a weaving of experiences and events creating a series of small wake-up calls. If I don't honor the message, then comes a crisis so big that only God could have orchestrated it to get my attention.

Even though my speaking business was prospering, something was stirring in my soul about wanting to live on a deeper level.

In fall 2011 a friend I'll call Grace insisted I come to Boone near the mountains of North Carolina to see some health providers who had helped her a lot. However, on the day of the appointment my gut was screaming at me, saying stay home, but I did not honor guidance. It was the Tuesday before Thanksgiving, and I was getting ready to go into a demanding three-day holiday market that weekend and I had many preparations to make.

The trip was disappointing, and I was waiting to hear from my friend about where I was supposed to go spend the night. I felt strongly that I should take the next exit and have a snack and wait there until my friend and I could connect.

Highway 421 was maddening because cars and trucks were racing 70 to 80 miles an hour by me. I noticed a lull ahead, which turned out to be an accident, so I completely stopped my car but looked in the rear view window to see a truck speeding towards me. Out of fear I put my left foot on the brake as well as the right to prevent my hitting other cars. My body tensed in fight or flight position, but nothing could stop the truck from plowing into me and then my colliding with the sports utility vehicle in front of me.

The driver of the truck was cited for hitting both vehicles. The front and back ends of my car were destroyed leaving me alive between the two barriers.

The next day I awoke in agony. I went to a chiropractor and described acute pain all over my body. After several sessions during the next week, she said I displayed the symptoms of costochondritis, an inflammation of the cartilage that attaches the ribs to the breastbone.

Due to my swollen feet and sore toes my shoes felt tight so I bought a pair of boots and tennis shoes in a larger size. While dealing with persistent pain and being unable to stand on my feet, I cancelled holiday shows and other book signings during my best sales season. This began my decline in income.

Suddenly my life revolved around appointments with health professionals to soothe the discomfort. My routine was scattered by phone calls related to insurance claims and car replacement concerns. The liability claims adjuster for the other driver's insurance company reassured me that all my medical bills would be paid.

Pain in both legs and right side continued to plague my days. When I climbed the steps in my house I felt like an old woman. If I didn't walk and stretch every day I became too stiff to function.

Every day I soaked in Epsom salt and baking soda to relieve the aches, used a heating pad and electric massager, and was forced to take high dosages of Ibuprofen. Several times a week I had appointments with body workers, including chiropractic adjustments and massage therapy.

Injuries from the car accident and treatment of pain dramatically changed my life…limiting my mobility, exhausting my energy, draining my imagination, stealing my time, and straining my finances.

Treatment for Pain Continues

After the holidays I decided to create another draft of my manuscript *Going Crazy*, now subtitled *Risking It All for Reinvention*. This project would nourish my soul and feed my pocketbook. However, sitting at the computer for long intervals was impossible. I discovered that using a stool to elevate my feet while typing helped, but the discomfort robbed me of my creative juices. As the pain plagued my focus I felt more and more invisible in terms of showing up in any area of my life, both personally and professionally.

I continued to focus on getting rid of the pain. I switched to a different massage therapist for MyoKinesthetic treatment. This healing system was created by a chiropractor, Dr. Michael Uriarte, to ease and eliminate pain, to restore range of motion, and to improve posture.

By now I was honoring the best of modern medicine with annual physical examinations. As the pain got worse instead of better I went to my doctor's office for a checkup. Blood tests showed a high score for Rheumatoid Arthritis (RA), which can be triggered by a car accident.

During my annual physical a spot showed up on my chest x-ray and doctor was concerned that it could be AAA (abdominal aortic aneurysm), which could explain some of the pain. We discussed whether the seat belt against me during car accident could have caused the AAA. She ordered a CT scan at UNC Hospital and set up an appointment with a doctor who specializes in vascular and heart problems. Fortunately, the CT scan did not indicate AAA, but that was a big scare!

I had avoided all prescription medicine since 1975, but the family nurse practitioner insisted I take Celebrix and Gabapentine and suggested I be fitted for constriction stockings. Taking the drugs and wearing these compression hose helped tremendously.

My doctor's office also set up appointments with a neurologist who could not offer answers and a rheumatologist who said I definitely had some form of myalgia and suggested I get treatment from an acupuncturist. I started seeing a practitioner who was certified to do physical therapy and acupuncture and got good results.

In summer 2014 I started receiving treatment from a different chiropractor who specializes in quantum healing. During the first visit he commented: "You are trying to drive a car with two flat tires." Many sessions later my legs were functioning much better.

Meanwhile the representative for the other driver's insurance company made me a low offer, which did not even cover medical bills. I was forced to secure the services of an attorney who filed lawsuit against the driver of the truck. So far, a year later, he has been unable to get my health expenses paid or obtain any reimbursement for pain and suffering and loss of income.

During this time I did business consulting for a client who would not listen to my advice and disregarded my years of experience in marketing. By now, my self-esteem had hit rock bottom, and I could only surrender my situation to God. While 2014 was the most challenging year of my life I am grateful to God for allowing me to learn new lessons in peace and prosperity that are growing my harvest everyday.

Understanding Spiritual Healing

During the many months of dealing with physical pain I took a deeper look at the mental and emotional trauma I was feeling and longed to get rid of the nightmares about seeing the truck coming towards me. I increased my practice of breathing techniques, visualization, meditation, prayer, and experimented with EFT (Emotional Freedom Technique) for releasing trauma.

While improving myself physically and mentally, I also renewed myself spiritually. I attended more church services, read more inspirational books, and drew upon encouraging verses from *The Bible*. My favorite is from Isaiah 40:31: "But they that wait upon the Lord shall renew their strength; they shall mount up with wings as eagles; they shall run, and not be weary; and they shall walk, and not faint."

I began to read a lot about spiritual and energetic healing. I especially enjoyed learning from Caroline Myss, author of several books on health and spirituality that were also available on audiotape. I devoured everything she wrote or said.

My favorite books continue to be: *Anatomy of the Spirit: The Seven Stages of Power*; *Defy Gravity: Healing Beyond the Bounds of Reason and Healing*; and *Entering the Castle: Finding the Inner Path to God and Your Soul's Purpose.*

During this time I began to understand the creation of health on a much deeper level. I realized that I had to draw upon everything I had ever learned in terms on holistic healing and also gain some new knowledge and wisdom. Most importantly I had to learn to honor messages from my gut.

I loved reading this quote by Caroline Myss:

"We often hesitate to follow our intuition out of fear. Most usually, we are afraid of the changes in our own life that our actions will bring. Intuitive guidance, however, is all about change. It is energetic data ripe with the potential to influence the rest of the world. To fear change but to crave intuitive clarity is like fearing the cold, dark night while pouring water on the fire that lights your cave. An insight the size of a mustard seed is powerful enough to bring down a mountain-sized illusion that may be holding our lives together. Truth strikes without mercy. We fear our intuitions because we fear the transformational power within our revelations."

While releasing emotional baggage I received a book in the mail *Less Clutter More Life*, written by my friend Barbara Hemphill. With the growth of the internet came the need to eliminate digital clutter, but in the past few years, Barbara realized that "the true clutter that prevents people from accomplishing their work and enjoying their lives is the emotional and spiritual clutter."

She says life is not easy but "eliminating physical, digital, emotional and spiritual clutter enables you to control what you can control, so you can accept what you can't."

Barbara believes that eliminating clutter frees your mind to "uncover the true purpose in your life."

My many adventures into healing revealed to me that I must release the past and focus on creating an enjoyable present and expecting a fulfilling future. Finally three years after the car accident I began to notice that my body was working almost normally again. I began to feel well mentally, emotionally, and spiritually.

Ongoing Health Strategies

Today I feel energetic, excited, and optimistic about the present and the future.

Therefore I must share the strategies that keep me feeling healthier and happier:

1. I drink lots of pure water every day. I mix coconut and/or almond milk with protein powder and also prepare smoothies in my blender made from raw greens and fruits.
2. I eat nutritious foods, including raw vegetables and fruits every day.
3. I curtail my intake of sugar and salt and avoid processed food and have totally eliminated foods with gluten.
4. I take nutritional supplements, herbal remedies, and homeopathic medicine and avoid prescription drugs.

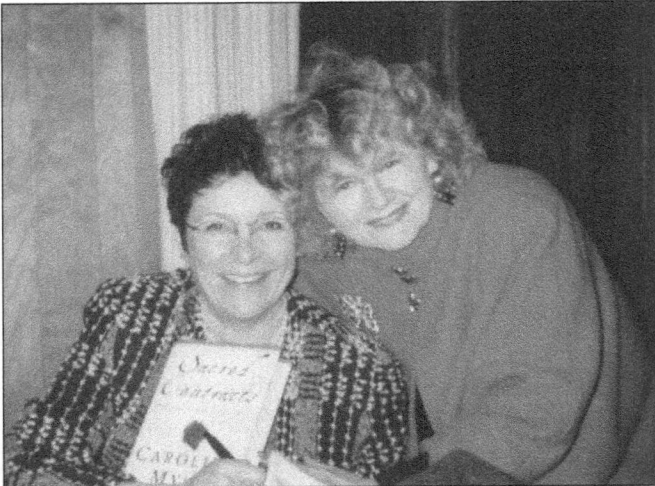

AlexSandra socializes with her favorite author and speaker
Caroline Myss at a book-signing

5. I move my body every day, usually in the form of walking, sometimes stretching and doing yoga. I vow to get back into dancing more this year.

6. Often I go outside and relish the healing rays of sunshine and enjoy the colors of nature. On warm days I take much longer walks and catch up on phone calls to friends.

7. Every day I soak in the tub with Epsom salt and/or baking soda to draw out toxins and soothe my body;

8. I get sufficient rest, and even though I don't sleep well some nights I take a nap most afternoons.

9. I pray, meditate, and often read spiritually uplifting articles and books.

10. I maintain a positive attitude.

11. I surround myself with loving family members and friends and supportive clients/customers – and avoid the ones who do not honor me.

12. I forgive the people who hurt me. I let go and let God.

As I have learned to integrate the healing of body, mind, and spirit, I am grateful to feel good again. I look forward to living longer and most importantly, dancing for the rest of my life.

Holistic Healing and Wholistic Work
are soul mates and spiritual guides
for creating fulfillment.
Combining both promotes a zeal
for laboring, loving, and living.

Writing From My Soul

During the New Year period and my birthday season every February I always consider possibilities for transforming body, mind, and spirit. Every January I reread *The Artist's Way, A Spiritual Path to Higher Creativity*, written by Julia Cameron with Mark Bryan and published in 1992. Believing that creative expression is the natural direction of life, the authors lead readers through a comprehensive 12-week program to recover their creativity from a variety of blocks, including limiting beliefs, fear, self-sabotage, guilt, addictions, and jealousy.

The first step in the program is to write by long hand three pages every morning – called "morning pages" – because this exercise allows the participant to dump junk out of the mind and to release trivia that is bogging down the brain. It is important not to judge the material no matter how bad because this is not literature but therapy! This technique opens up possibilities for exciting ideas and eventually makes writing habitual and ultimately creative.

In 2015 I searched for another book that would feed my spirit and found *Writing Down Your Soul: How to Activate and Listen to the Extraordinary Voice Within*, written by Janet Conner and published in 2008. Janet started journaling in 1996 when she was threatened by domestic violence and desperately searching for a way out of her misery. Like millions of others, Janet read *The Artist's Way* and realized the power of writing every day.

For author Janet Conner writing three pages was not enough. By writing about 30 pages in the form of a letter to God she released negative feelings, forgave the people who had hurt her, and began to tune into her Higher Self.

Janet felt that God was actually responding to her questions and offering solutions to her problems. The more time Janet spent writing the more she overcame overwhelming circumstances and moved forward to forgiveness, healing, joy, and deliverance.

As I reviewed the tools I have used in the past to deal with challenges in my life, I recalled that even as a child writing became my outlet for venting my frustrations, releasing pain, and expressing creativity. Throughout my life writing had allowed me to support myself financially, but most importantly writing had stirred my soul, given me a sense of purpose, and made life rewarding.

So, if you are facing challenges in your life, pick up a pen and paper and start writing – and ask yourself:

1. What am I feeling about this situation?
2. What message is there in this for me?
3. What solutions or new ways of responding to life might I discover in this process?

While there are many approaches to connecting with your Higher Self and communicating with God....praying, meditating, being with nature, having healing sessions...writing is an easy way to have a vibrant conversation with the wisdom that dwells in your consciousness.

For several months I honored this soul writing ritual every morning, and this stimulated my creative juices so I started creating exciting newspaper columns. Eventually I felt led to go through about 100 articles I had written in recent years to see if they could become chapters in a manuscript.

Returning to Wholistic Work

Like with our health, our work must be about healing our lives as well as our bodies, renewing our minds, and feeding our spirits more so than about making money. Healthy and happy people create more harmony in their homes and work environments.

I believe that Wholistic Work refers to our Work in this society being an integration of our calling, our caring, our talents, our skills, our passion, and our purpose while also meeting the needs of others who learn from our gifts. Wholistic Work is a labor of love and a love of labor because it touches our heart and stirs our soul.

Our work must stimulate self-expression, ignite our creativity, and enhance our zest for living. At best work is about loving labor, serving our sense of meaning, honoring our purpose, and manifesting our mission in this society and on this planet.

Can our avocation become an exciting vocation?
Can our passion lead us to a fulfilling career?
Can our compassion create a form of ministry?
Can our core values motivate us professionally as well as personally to contribute to society in a deeper way?

Holistic Healing and Wholistic Work are soul mates and spiritual guides for creating fulfillment. Combining both promotes a zeal for laboring, loving, and living.

Every day I reassess the strategies and incorporate the disciplines required for living in harmony with holistic healing and Wholistic Work, and I also experience the joys and relish the rewards.

Creating a New Book

In 2015 I began to bring wholeness and holism again to my work…remembering the obsession with Wholistic Work that guided me to find my authentic voice as a writer in that cabin 17 years ago. Back then writing three drafts of *Going Crazy…Getting Sane* healed something in me. I know what it is like to go crazy and to get sane, but somehow that title did not seem right for a book that longed to be born. I have not published that book but it has been worth $50,000 in therapy!

Through the months, I considered titles like *Risking It All for Reinvention, A Time to Soar*, and *Awaken the Butterfly Within* for my evolving manuscript, but I did not feel connected to any name. While visiting a close friend Jane, we discussed ideas about the manuscript, and she noted that I am always learning lessons and sharing my experiences through writing and speaking. So the subtitle became *Timeless Lessons for an Abundant Life*. However, I simply could not come up with the main title.

While I pray and meditate a lot, I had not consulted with God for input on the book's name. That night I went to bed and asked for the perfect title. As I awoke in the morning I heard the harvest clear as a bell. I spoke the words out loud…*The Harvest*…and then I felt cold chills all over my body. This was the ideal name for my current book.

Once I knew the name of my baby in the womb it was easier to discover how what I had written already would fit in the theme and what needed to be created to make my child ready to be born. I had learned many, many lessons from my experiences.

The Harvest describes my progress on this planet. My life has been about sowing and reaping, starting with growing up on a farm and drawing upon all the components from sowing seeds to bringing forth fresh fruits and vegetables to the kitchen and to harvesting crops for our use and to take to the marketplace. Later, I continued sowing and reaping and expecting harvests with a communications career in writing, editing, marketing, public relations, publishing, and promoting products and services. Working with media outlets – newspapers, magazines, television and radio stations – and online internet sites I have experienced short-term and long-range results from the ongoing cycle of sowing seeds and producing harvest after harvest.

Nothing is wasted on the farm, and this is true of all aspects in life. Even when dead plants are plowed back into the ground this compost adds nutrient to the ground. When crops are rotated the new plants require different substances from the soil for nourishment.

In my life I have realized that every pain will lead to gain...everything that seems bad can eventually lead to goodness.

So with this book I come back home to my greatest gift...and return to the way of the writer. My focus on speaking had been wonderful but obviously God was calling me to a higher level of writing and speaking so I could be of greater service to others. I am a writer who speaks to others through words on paper or spoken sentences.

This is the work I know best…to write, to publish, to promote, to reinvent, to share insights from experiences that hurt my body, upset my mind, and sometimes break my spirit. Now it is time for me to allow writing to heal my soul and restore my career.

On Fourth of July I claimed this book, *The Harvest*, as my Declaration of Independence from the old life and the beginning of freedom to live up to the highest potential of holistic healing and Wholistic Work. Obviously I am finding a unique voice beyond nostalgia that ignites my creativity and feeds my spirit and ultimately will bring forth my truth and shed light to others.

In this book I have shared timeless lessons from my country childhood – being raised on a big farm across the road from Grandpa's country store – and insights I have gained throughout my "citified" communications career that have helped me and can inspire readers and audiences. My intention is to offer ideas for growing an abundant life filled with health, happiness, peace, and prosperity.

An abundant life is about learning timeless lessons and expecting a harvest…

Lessons Learned

When you stray so far off of God's Path that you aren't listening to His Guidance, you will experience an intervention to help realign you to the path!

True healing brings together the best tools and methodologies to honor our physical bodies, our emotional selves and our spiritual selves.

It is almost impossible to access and utilize our creativity when we are in pain at the physical, emotional or spiritual level. We must take care of and honor ourselves in order to successfully do the work God has called us to do.

Questions

What kind of wake-up calls or shake-ups have you experienced that could be calling you to a Higher Purpose?

Where have you allowed fear, anger, resentment, guilt or limiting beliefs to stop you from doing what you feel in your heart you should be doing?

Are you willing to learn the lessons necessary to create harvest after harvest in your life?

AlexSandra strolls through a field of milo, a grain sorghum
now grown on the Lett family farm in North Carolina.
The new crop indicates reinvention continues to take place
in farming as well as all areas of life.

Acknowledgements to Mighty Fine Folks

When seeking a new voice as a writer in 2000 I started creating nostalgic articles for newspapers in the Wilmington and Sanford areas of North Carolina. Drawing upon the idea of growing up in Buckhorn community where we used to "set" around at my Grandpa's country store I called the column "Lett's Set a Spell." The popularity of the column has led to the publication of several books and creation of audio CDs. Now this manuscript celebrates the 15th anniversary of sharing stories and offering reflections on a way of working and living through several generations.

While writing the column every week I have been blessed with guidance and comments from David Clegg, Jane Norton, Lynn Garren Henderson, and Tracey Daley Brocker through the years. Also I have received lots of ongoing feedback from Peggy Makepeace, Linda Gruenfeld, Jackie Parker, and Patricia Mabe.

The visual conception team for my products has always included my artist friend Susan Beal, photographer Jimmy Haire, and graphic designers Roxanne Miller-Simeone and Renay Wulpern of Jones Printing in Sanford.

The original idea for this book was conceived in the mid-1990s when I experienced a major career and life reassessment. In 1998 I wrote a manuscript called *Going Crazy...Getting Sane* about reinventing ourselves, and that book has gone through many drafts but is not ready to be born.

In 2015, while exploring the themes of more than 100 columns, I thought I was writing a self-help book *Risking It All for Reinvention*. However, as this manuscript evolved, I enrolled in a memoir workshop series offered by poet and teacher Alice Osborn in Raleigh and was reminded that my style of writing includes parables that teach others.

When brainstorming with my friend Jane Norton we decided that my gift is learning lessons and then providing insights with my readers and audiences. Our discussion led to the creation of a possible sub-title, *Timeless Lessons for an Abundant Life*. While struggling to decide on a main title for my new book I asked God for guidance. Sure enough the next morning I awoke and heard the words "the harvest" and then with cold chills I said my child's name *The Harvest*.

In writing this version of the book I have been supported by a team of mid-wives including Alice Osborn, Debra May, Jane Norton, Sheyenne Kreamer, Tracey Daley Brocker, Peggy Makepeace, Lynn Garren Henderson, Kerry Ahrend, Sally Hanson, Michelle Rogers, Lynn Davis, Jinger Gibson, Chancy Kapp, and many others. I have received great ideas from marketing and publishing experts Diana M. Needham and Kevin Snyder.

Family members who assisted are Michael Yarborough, Mary Wilson-Wittenstrom, Betty Taylor Wade, Carolyn Lett McNeill, Sharon Wood Lett, Tony and Rozie Leone Lett, Art and Janice Lett Coleman. Soul sisters who are always sending love and light are Donna Dutton, Deb Mangis, Judy Fourie, Diana Hales, Arya Heath, Marj Marie, Glenda Westbrook-Neilsen, Joann Abbott Thaxton, Margie Brache, Barbara Hemphill, Judy Olsen Womack, Judi Price Womack, Jane McPhaul, Helen Yarborough Maddox, Lois Thomas, Carolyn Grant, Sheila Hale Ogle, Darleen Johns, Lana Calloway and Leslie Flowers. Special thanks to Don Westbrook and the late George Ward for their energy.

I relish the ongoing support of the folks at *The Sanford Herald,* Including Bill Horner, general manager, and R.V. Hight who allow me to run my column every Sunday in its newspaper and other publications that have featured my articles.

In all my activities I am assisted by my fabulous friend Deborah Harrell Meehan, founder of the Wild Wacky Wonderful Women of the World, based in Raleigh, and its members who encourage me in so many ways.

I am very thankful for many mighty fine folks helping me in numerous ways – it would require a book just to discuss these individuals and their contributions to my life. I am blessed constantly by my furry feline friends King Khaki, Prince Charming, Princess Joy, and Silver Queen who offer unconditional love and healing hugs.

With the release of **The Harvest** I am especially grateful for all the people who have provided guidance in my journey to live in harmony with holistic healing and what I call "Wholistic Work." With this book I offer a humble appreciation for the lessons I have learned and pray that they will inspire others to experience greater health, happiness, peace, and prosperity.

Lett's Set a Spell
with
AlexSandra "Sandy Lynn" Lett

Like most Southern girls AlexSandra Lett was referred to by a double name. As "Sandy Lynn" she grew up writing, singing, dramatizing, dancing, and avoiding chores on a big farm in the Buckhorn community of Lee County in rural North Carolina.

At an early age she took a fancy to the written word and served as editor of her high school newspaper. She attended Sandhills Community College in Pinehurst, North Carolina, then received a distinguished journalism scholarship at the University of North Carolina at Chapel Hill. She later pursued graduate studies in communications at N.C. State University in Raleigh. This country girl became "citified" for a while, and according to her family, "educated beyond her intelligence."

For several years AlexSandra wrote a weekly newspaper column called "Natural Living," which established her as an expert on healing body, mind, and spirit. She published a book **Natural Living:** *From Stress to Rest* in 1984.

After working in the media – newspapers, magazines and television – AlexSandra L. Lett founded a company, ALL Communications, in Raleigh in 1991. Her business offered writing, editing, marketing, public relations, and professional speaking services. Soon afterwards she created TRANSFORMATIONS as a vehicle for offering programs related to personal and professional excellence, including such topics as, releasing stress, increasing energy, creating success, and managing change.

In spring 2000 AlexSandra started writing humorous articles featuring saucy stories and colorful characters from her Grandpa's country store for publications and websites. The popularity of her "Lett's Set a Spell" column led to the publication of *A Timeless Place*, *Lett's Set a Spell at the Country Store*. AlexSandra continued with nostalgia offerings, including *Timeless Moons*, *Seasons of the Fields and Matters of the Heart* and *Timeless Recipes and Remedies*, *Country Cooking, Customs, and Cures* and *Coming Home to my Country Heart*, *Timeless Reflections on Work, Family, Health, and Spirit*. In addition to inspiring readers AlexSandra shares entertaining anecdotes and interesting reflections with appreciative audiences.

Through her company Southern Books & Talks AlexSandra offers keynotes, seminars, workshops, and "funshops" on various topics, including Going Crazy… Getting Sane, "Set a Spell" at the Country Store, Lessons from the Farm, It's Never Too Late to Have a Happy Childhood, Doing What You Love and Making Money Too, and Transforming Mind, Body, and Spirit. Using her natural Southern accent and wearing her aunt's 1968 Easter frock AlexSandra creates an alter-ego "Sandy Lynn" and presents compelling programs that tickle the funny bone, soften the heart, and speak to the soul.

For more information about speaking engagements by the author contact:

AlexSandra "Sandy Lynn" Lett

919-258-9299

TRANSFORMATIONS

1996 Buckhorn Road
Sanford, NC 27330-9782   USA
LettsSetaSpell@aol.com
www.atimelessplace.com

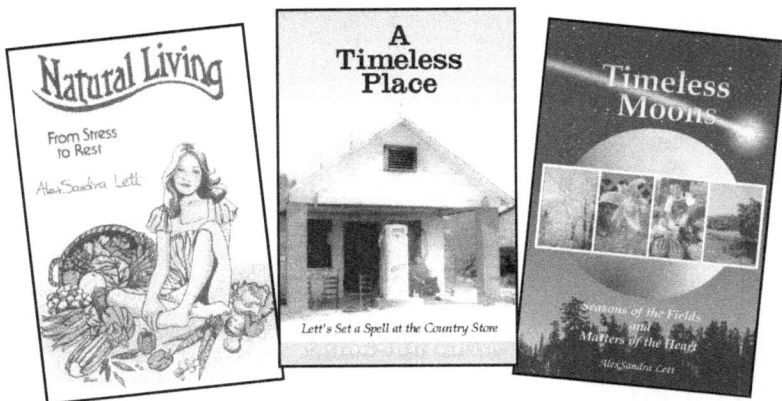

Natural Living, *From Stress to Rest* opens with the author's search for a cure from a serious illness. She describes symptoms of disease and dis-ease she wants to heal and aspects of stress people need to avoid. The second part focuses on ways to move from stress to rest and even to best. As a pioneer in holistic approaches the author discusses many ideas to healing body, mind, and spirit, including food as medicine, vitamins, minerals, enzymes, and herbs. The book ends with AlexSandra's discovery of health. (Published in 1984 - out of print)

A Timeless Place, *Lett's Set a Spell at the Country Store* focuses on an era when the country store was the social center of a community. It features colorful characters who live forever through entertaining anecdotes about love and war, courting, farming, fishing, quilting, hog-killing, party lines, radio shows, and the best about country living and giving.

Timeless Moons, *Seasons of the Fields and Matters of the Heart* features stories about relying on *The Farmers Almanac* and popular folklore to plant crops, make soap, cut hair, chop wood, and catch fish. Other topics relating to rural culture include Moonshine and stock car racing; MoonPies and RC Colas; country customs and timeless traditions.

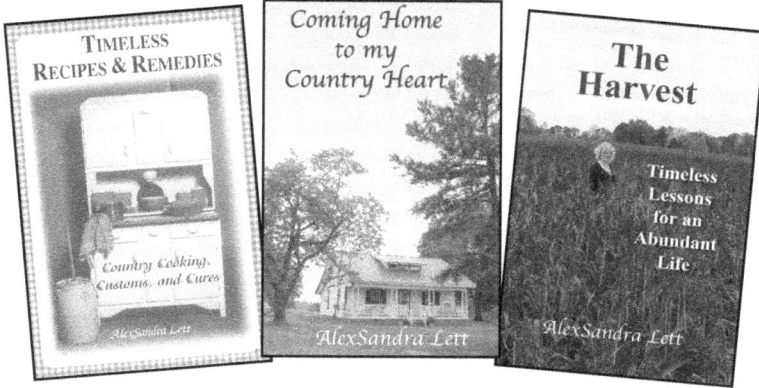

Timeless Recipes and Remedies, *Country Cooking, Customs, and Cures* captures the enticing aromas and delicious flavors of favorites ranging from hard-to-find recipes from a rural kitchen in the 1920s to modern culinary creations. The book explores common sense cures from Grandma's cupboard, healing aids from Grandpa's country store, and other folklore favorites.

Coming Home to my Country Heart, *Timeless Reflections on Work, Family, Health, and Spirit* explores the author's shift from president of a communications company in the city to a writer living in the country and discovering her unique voice. She returns to her home community, deals with the decline and death of both parents, and begins to truly honor her deep roots.

The Harvest, *Timeless Lessons for an Abundant Life* features penetrating anecdotes and profound insights from the author's country childhood and "citified" communications career that will help readers create an abundant life filled with health, happiness, peace, and prosperity. Growing up on a big farm across the road from her Grandpa's country store, "Sandy Lynn" learned lessons that helped her later to succeed in business, in the arts, and in life.

All books are available in easy-to-read print.
For more information contact 919-258-9299 or LettsSetaSpell@aol.com.
Visit www.atimelessplace.com

ORDER FORM for books written by
AlexSandra "Sandy Lynn" Lett

A Timeless Place
Lett's Set a Spell at the Country Store
6" x 9"Hardcover, 175 pages   Retail $19.95   _____
ISBN-13: 978-0-9613649-6-0
4 Compact Disc Set – 5 hours read by author   Retail $21.95   _____
ISBN-13: 978-0-9613649-3-9

Timeless Moons
Seasons of the Fields and Matters of the Heart
6" x 9"Hardcover, 175 pages   Retail $19.95   _____
ISBN-13: 978-0-9613649-5-3

Timeless Recipes and Remedies
Country Cooking, Customs, and Cures
6" x 9"Hardcover, 221 pages   Retail $ 21.95   _____
ISBN-13: 978-0-9613649-9-1

Coming Home to my Country Heart
Timeless Reflections on Work, Family, Health, and Spirit
6" x 9"Hardcover, 127 pages   Retail $15.95   _____
ISBN-13: 978-0-9613649-8-4

The Harvest
Timeless Lessons for an Abundant Life
6" x 9"Hardcover, 151 pages   Retail $19.95   _____
ISBN-13: 978-0-9970324-1-3
6" x 9"Paperback, 151 pages   Retail $14.95   _____
ISBN-13: 978-0-9970324-2-0

Books and Kindle edition available at Amazon.com

SUB TOTAL   _____

7% sales tax for NC residents   _____

Book Rate shipping/handling
    $4 for first book, $2 extra for each additional book   _____
Gift orders for single autograped books may be
shipped directly to recipients at priority mail rates
    $6 for first book, $2 extra for each additional book   _____

TOTAL AMOUNT   _____

To order books call 919-258-9299 or send a check or money order to
Southern Books & Talks, 1996 Buckhorn Rd., Sanford, NC 27330-9782

Name _____

Address _____

Phone Number _____E-mail Address_____

Credit Card Number _____Expiration Date _____

Names to be used for autographed copies _____